URGINGS

OF THE HEART

URGINGS
OF THE HEART

A Spirituality of Integration

WILKIE AU AND NOREEN CANNON

PAULIST PRESS
New York/Mahwah, N.J.

Quotations from the following articles are used with permission:

"Knowing Your Shadow" in *Human Development*
by Noreen Cannon (Fall, 1985).
"Envy: A Longing for Wholeness" in *Human Development*
by Noreen Cannon (Fall, 1991).
"From Codependency to Contemplation" in *Human Development*
by Noreen Cannon and Wilkie Au (Summer, 1991).
"The Plague of Perfectionism" in *Human Development*
by Noreen Cannon and Wilkie Au (Fall, 1992).
"Greeting the Shadow that Lives Down the Road" in *Psychological Perspectives*
(Issue 27, Fall/Winter 1994).

Library of Congress Cataloging-in-Publication Data

Au, Wilkie,   1944-
Urgings of the heart : a spirituality of integration / Wilkie Au
and Noreen Cannon.
p.   cm.
Includes bibliographical references.
ISBN 0-8091-3604-X (alk. paper)
1. Spiritual life. 2. Psychology and religion. 3. Perfection—
Religious aspects—Christianity. 4. Perfectionism (Personality
trait) I. Cannon, Noreen, 1945-   . II. Title.
BV4501.2.A84   1995   95-35391
248.4'82—dc20   CIP

Published by Paulist Press
997 Macarthur Boulevard
Mahwah, New Jersey 07430

Printed and bound in the
United States of America

CONTENTS

248
q 6

v

108931

ACKNOWLEDGMENTS

JOINT AUTHORSHIP has made this work a collaborative effort from start to finish. However, the circle of collaboration extends far beyond the two authors. Many friends and colleagues have contributed through their encouragement and feedback. We are happy to thank and acknowledge them here.

We thank Jean Bloomquist, Kay Cannon, Robert Caro, S.J., and Miriam Therese Larkin, C.S.J. for their careful reading of the entire manuscript and for their perceptive comments and suggestions. To Jerry McKevitt, S.J., and Earl Kofler, Ph.D., we are grateful for their helpful remarks on portions of the text.

We thank Janet Duffy, C.S.J. for her help with the cover design. The "yin-yang" symbol of wholeness placed together with the Cross reflects our belief that psychological and spiritual growth go hand in hand. We are also grateful to the many participants of the workshops that we have conducted throughout the United States and Canada. Their feedback and enthusiastic response motivated us to write this book.

We are indebted to Lore Zeller, proofreader for *Psychological Perspectives*, for her care and generosity in reviewing the proofpages.

Portions of some chapters have appeared in somewhat different form in *Human Development*. We thank the editors for their permission to include those materials here.

Last and by no means least, we are grateful to our families and friends for their ongoing love and support.

W. W. A.
Loyola Marymount University

N. D. C.
C. G. Jung Institute
Los Angeles

The greatest problem lies in trying to integrate everything, to invest all with meaning, see it all as part of a larger, more meaningful life.

—Hildegard of Bingen

INTRODUCTION

HE COULD HARDLY believe it. He now sat in the peaceful solitude of his own room, comforted by the nearby sounds of warm conversation flowing from the kitchen. But just two brief days ago, he was literally among the dead, tormented by his own fragmented spirit and chained to the rocks in the cemetery at the outskirts of town. He remembered clearly how out of control he was: howling like a madman, smashing himself with self-destructive blows, and splintered into so many warring parts inside that when the man named Jesus of Nazareth asked who he was, he could only screech out a loud and terrifying, "My name is Legion!" What a frightening experience that was. Yet, to his surprise, Jesus was not scared off but stayed on—to help him face the agony of his inner division with compassionate understanding, to melt his self-hatred with the warmth of his touch. Encountering Jesus in this way made all the difference in the world. Even the crowd that gathered was amazed by the change in him as he sat in their midst, now well-dressed and in his full senses. But the onlookers could only get a glimmer of what took place the day Jesus entered his life. Even now, as he ruminated over what had happened, his mind was only slowly grasping the impact of that transforming experience. Not only did he feel that he was made whole by Jesus, given a unified sense of himself, but he also felt deep in his soul that the touch of Jesus had marked him for life as one called to be holy and as one empowered to love others as Jesus had loved him.

The story of "Legion," the Gerasene demoniac cured by Jesus (Mk 5:1-20), raises an important question: Is there a connection between psychological health and spiritual development, between wholeness and holiness? Today, this question sparks off lively debate and widely divergent opinions. Some people are suspicious of psychology and see it as a danger to spiritual development and irrelevant to loving like Christ. A variety of Christian fundamentalists, for instance, argue that the pursuit of psychological health not only distracts but also endangers the sole important task of saving one's soul. Others

1

are critical of religion and point out how faith systems can be abusive, wounding people psychologically and emotionally, thereby impairing our ability to love.[1] A third point of view is expressed by Ruth Burrows, a contemporary spiritual writer, who argues that "God is not glorified by half-persons."[2] With these provocative words, she voices the belief that psychological and spiritual growth are tightly linked. Her words echo the sentiments of St. Irenaeus, a father of the second-century church, who stated that "the glory of God is the human person fully alive."[3] The insights of Burrows and Irenaeus capture the religious significance of the human longing for wholeness. Wholeness is not our idea; it is God's. The urgings of the heart that impel us to grow and become fully who we are reflect God's desire to be uniquely incarnated in each of us.

The theme of this book is that spiritual and psychological growth go hand in hand. Neither a spirituality that ignores the dynamics of psychological growth nor a psychology that denies the spiritual nature of the human person can serve as an adequate guide today for people who seek to live with greater harmony and integration. The spirituality presented here is a holistic one in the sense that it recognizes the dynamic interrelation between our spiritual and psychological selves, between our quest for holiness and our desire for wholeness.

Holiness, strictly speaking, is an attribute of God, who alone is the "wholly Other," to whom all created beings owe their existence and grateful adoration. Yet the Bible exhorts us to strive for holiness by imitating the love of God. In the Sermon on the Mount in Matthew's gospel, Jesus clearly sums up the goal of Christian life as loving as God does. This loving God causes the sun to rise on the bad as well as the good and the rain to fall on the honest and dishonest alike (5:45-46). In brief, Jesus states that we are to become holy as God is holy by loving in an inclusive and all-embracing way. Christian holiness, then, entails continually expanding the boundaries of our hearts so that more and more people—even though unrelated to us by blood, belief, or national boundaries—can find in us a caring place. Put concretely, as Christians grow in holiness, their "enemy list" grows shorter and their Christmas list grows longer.

This inclusive love also challenges us to make friends with those hidden parts of ourselves that we have come to consider as enemies. Thus, the call to holiness is also a call to wholeness. As the story of the Gerasene demoniac shows, inner divisions and brokenness can stand in the way of our loving others. While we do not know the details of this man's past, we see the results: he is imprisoned by it, so paralyzed by inner turmoil and pain that he can neither reach out to others nor allow others to touch him. In our own lives, a history of emotional deprivation or abuse may have saddled us with patterns of thinking, feeling, and behaving that once helped us survive a dysfunctional family situation but now sabotage our efforts to develop intimate relationships as adults. Or we may find that inner conflicts and struggles deplete our outer-directed energy for loving others. Lack of self-love and the resulting self-rejection impede loving because what we cannot accept in ourselves we invariably reject in others. In these and many other ways, what divides us from ourselves also separates us from God and others.

Spiritual transformation consists of two movements: self-appropriation and self-transcendence. Self-appropriation involves self-knowledge and self-understanding. Practically, it means knowing what is going on inside ourselves: knowing who we are, knowing why we choose what we choose, why we do what we do and what our feelings and desires are. In other words, self-appropriation requires a habit of self-reflection that attunes us to the currents and undercurrents of our lives. Self-transcendence, on the other hand, refers to the gradual transformation of our ego-centered vision and choices so that they become God-centered. This movement has two aspects. First, it involves developing an intimate relationship with God and a willingness to share in the ministry of Jesus today by embodying the compassion of God for others. Second, it calls us to deepen our ability to discern God's will for us and a willingness to do it, confident that it is God's work and that God gives us the grace to do it.

Our whole life as Christians involves ongoing conversion in both areas. In the past, there has been a tendency to devalue self-appropriation. Some forms of spirituality have been overly suspicious of psychology and the kind of introspection it generates, fearing that it would turn us too much in on ourselves, making us self-centered rather than other-centered. A holistic spirituality recognizes the equal importance and complementarity of self-appropriation and self-transcendence. The dynamic of Christian love is to move beyond self-concern and to reach out to God and others in compassion and care. Yet this outreach needs always to be open to a purification that keeps it as free as possible from subtle self-seeking and egotistical gratifications. Psychological integration is not meant to substitute for altruistic love. Rather, the insights of psychology can be used by us as Christians to illumine and support our vocation to love as Jesus did. While this book focuses on self-appropriation, it is always in the light of how self-knowledge fosters genuine self-transcendence. Self-transcendence, the gift of self to God and others, is the hunger of our being.

Chapter One is like the overture to a musical. It highlights the importance of self-knowledge for spiritual and psychological growth and introduces themes that will be developed at greater length later in the book. Chapters Two through Six deal with some of the major impediments to our growth in holiness and wholeness today: the shadow (Chapter Two), codependency (Chapter Three), perfectionism (Chapter Four), envy (Chapter Five), and overwork (Chapter Six). While treating a variety of topics, these chapters are all variations of a central theme: as consciousness of ourselves and others expands, so will our development as persons made to love and be loved. The final two chapters deal with the part that intimate relationships (Chapter Seven), compassion and collaboration (Chapter Eight) can contribute to the wholeness we seek.

A story from the work of Jesuit Anthony de Mello captures the spirit and message of this book.

> Even though it was the Master's Day of Silence, a traveler begged for a word of wisdom that would guide him through life's journey.
>
> The Master nodded affably, took a sheet of paper and wrote a single word on it: "Awareness."
>
> The visitor was perplexed. "That's too brief. Would you please expand on it a bit?"
>
> The Master took the paper back and wrote: "Awareness, awareness, awareness."
>
> "But what do those words *mean*?" said the stranger helplessly.
>
> The Master reached out for the paper and wrote: "Awareness, awareness, awareness means AWARENESS."[4]

This story reflects our understanding of spirituality as a continual process of being aware, of seeing, of becoming conscious.

The holistic Christian spirituality contained in these pages is rooted in a belief in God's all-embracing love for each of us just as we are, with all the positive and negative aspects that make us richly complex and unique individuals. Like the mother hen that gathers all her chicks under her wings, God's love encompasses each of us with warm acceptance. Our spiritual challenge is simply to receive God's affirming love as an unearned gift. Living in an achievement-oriented society, many of us are influenced by an achievement-oriented spirituality, in which there is no place for receiving. We resist being indebted and insist on working for whatever we get. This attitude stands in the way of our receiving from God, who continually invites us to draw near to obtain what we need: "Oh, come to the water, all you who are thirsty; though you have no money, come! Buy corn without money, and eat, and, at no cost, wine and milk.... Pay attention, come to me; listen, and your soul will live" (Is 55:1, 3). To listen to God's reassuring word of love gives us a sense of being whole and lovable, and frees us to love others in a way that resembles the love of God who alone is holy.

CHAPTER ONE

HOLISTIC SPIRITUALITY:
OUR HUNGER FOR WHOLENESS

*According to the riches of God's glory, may you have the power for
your hidden self to grow strong, so that Christ may dwell in your hearts
through faith and you may be filled with the utter fullness of God.*
EPHESIANS 3:16-19

IN HIS LETTER to the Romans, St. Paul paints a psychological self-
portrait that has become a classical illustration of our condition as
human beings. The passage has an enduring ring because its
description of Paul's inward struggle resonates deeply with the
personal experience of people throughout the ages. Like Paul, we
too live with a divided self. We encounter warring forces within
ourselves so strong and autonomous that we often feel helpless and
weak. Like Paul, we are perplexed by the mystery of our interior
fragmentation. When the apostle declares, "I cannot understand my
own behavior," we know what he means. "I fail to carry out the
things I want to do, and I find myself doing the very things I hate...
for though the will to do what is good is in me, the performance is
not, with the result that instead of doing the good things I want to
do, I carry out the sinful things I do not want.... What a wretch I
am!" (Rom 7:14-15, 18). The self-sabotaging self wages war within
every man and woman. That is why people everywhere hunger for
wholeness.

THE PARADOXICAL NATURE OF WHOLENESS

The pursuit of wholeness has frustrated many people in our culture because popular psychology has created an understanding of wholeness that is itself both incomplete and elusive. Wholeness has been presented as finally "getting it all together" in a steady state of total harmony and peace. This cultural notion of wholeness is attractive to many, because it promises something that is achievable in a once-and-for-all way, if only one discovers the right spiritual path, therapy, or guru.

The goal of wholeness as seen from the perspective of a holistic Christian spirituality differs drastically from this popular conception. Viewing wholeness in a paradoxical way, Christian spirituality associates it with a wholehearted commitment to "always being on the way" rather than "having it all together." A "whole" person values consciousness and is committed to being aware and reflective about how his or her actions, thoughts, and feelings affect the life of love to which Christians are called.

Paradox is an important way of understanding realities too complex to be explained from a single viewpoint. It allows us to "say the whole truth" by simultaneously juxtaposing two seemingly contradictory or conflicting assertions. Physicist Neils Bohr helps us appreciate paradox as a mode of knowing when he says, "The opposite of a true statement is a false statement, but the opposite of a profound truth can be another profound truth."[1] A proper understanding of Christian wholeness confronts us with several paradoxes. First, wholeness brings contentment and harmony into our lives; but dealing creatively with conflict, the shadow side of wholeness, will always be part of its reality. Because this paradoxical understanding of wholeness threatens the pleasurable anticipation of harmony, it has not caught the fancy of mass culture. "Wholeness without its shadow," asserts a Jungian thinker, "is very much the 'in thing' of the moment. Popular psychology has made it that way."[2] Second, instead of thinking complacently that they have it made, people who are whole are ever-faithful to the struggles of ongoing growth. Third, they consistently put serious effort into becoming whole, while acknowledging at the same time that, left to themselves, they cannot bring it about. Wholeness comes as a gift from a Power greater than themselves. Fourth, people striving to become whole are continually open to self-transcendence. They experience themselves as always on the verge of "something more" and believe that present struggles and difficulties are the threshold to new life and growth. This belief, of course, is rooted in the central paradox of Christian faith: the paschal mystery that life comes through death, that one gains oneself by losing oneself (Mk 8:35-36).

WHOLENESS AND SELF-TRANSCENDENCE

In the context of Christian development, self-transcendence contains two important meanings. First, a person who is open to self-transcendence is one who respects the mystery of his or her personhood, realizing that the richness of the self can never be entirely fathomed at any moment in time and that no self-image can adequately represent the reality of a self that has the potential for becoming more tomorrow than it is today. "God is always more" is an ancient theological axiom that cautions against reducing the ineffable mystery of God to puny human images. This axiom applies also to the mystery of the human person. Stalled and stale images of the self are ones that are outdated and rigid. Like a procrustean bed, these constrictive self-images force the unique self to fit into inflexible, ill-fitting categories. "That's just not me" and "That's the kind of person I am" are common expressions of self-images that stifle growth into wholeness, images that prematurely stop the flow of what is meant by God to be an ongoing process of self-formation. Fritz Perls, the founder of Gestalt Therapy, used to warn against confusing self-actualization, which is an open-ended and lifelong process, with *self-image* actualization, which is based on mistakenly identifying old pictures of the self taken at a certain period of time for the real, ever-unfolding self.

Second, a person who is open to self-transcendence is one who believes that grace abounds everywhere and that a dramatic in-breaking of God can occur at any moment, even as one paradoxically affirms that God is already present at every moment. Examples of such transcendent experiences are: peak experiences, as described by psychologist Abraham Maslow in his study of self-actualizing individuals; *kensho* or *nirvana*, moments of enlightenment spoken about in the literature of Zen meditation; and "consolation without previous cause," discussed by Ignatius of Loyola in his Rules of Discernment. That these diverse moments of self-transcendence share the common characteristic of providing a sense of wholeness can be perceived in the similar and interchangeable ways that these various experiences have been described: feeling a deep sense of being worthy, accepted, and loved; feeling at one with oneself, an inner harmony devoid of inner conflicts and divisions; feeling like one who is fully functioning or being in rare form; feeling at one with God and the universe as well as a deep solidarity with people throughout the world.

Those who have enjoyed these self-transcending experiences report that their altered state of consciousness is an instance of heightened awareness rather than a permanent condition. Like a flash of intuitive insight that suddenly clarifies how one must settle an important matter, or intense feelings of being loved by God that surge up without warning as one enjoys a sunset, these moments of self-transcendence are received as a gift, since those who have them realize that they did nothing consciously or deliberately to cause them. Furthermore, they are humbled in the knowledge that they do not possess within themselves the capacity to reduplicate them. All that is within their power is to create a disposition of openness and receptivity that allows them to be struck by an ecstatic grace that brings unity out of fragmentation. These moments are experienced as true blessings because they bestow a tangible and intense feeling of wholeness.

Spirituality as a Way to Self-Transcendence

The most traditional understanding of spirituality is that of a way or path that leads to self-transcendence. This notion is rooted in both Eastern and Western thought. Chinese philosophy speaks of the *tao*, or eternal pathway, leading to inner peace and harmony with others. In Japanese thought, the Chinese character *tao* is rendered *do*, as in *kyudo* (the way of archery), *kado* (the way of flower arrangement), and *chado* (the way of tea). These various Japanese arts are more than mere hobbies or avocations. They are spiritual disciplines designed to bring about not only internal harmony but also focused energy and unperturbed action in the outer world. Names of various Asian martial arts, like *judo* and *aikido*, indicate that these physical disciplines are meant not only to be systems of self-defense but also a comprehensive spiritual path for achieving harmony and dealing creatively with conflict. Thus, training in all these Japanese arts begins not with the practical skills of each discipline but with Zen meditation. It sometimes surprises students eager to learn the way of archery, tea, or the martial arts that a long period of *zazen*, or sitting meditation, is required before the aspiring disciple is initiated into a particular "way."

In the New Testament, spirituality as *a way* is a prominent metaphor describing the nature of Christian discipleship. The Acts of the Apostles reports that one of the first names given to Christians was "followers of the way" (Acts 9:2).[3] The "way section" of Mark's gospel best illustrates the early Christian community's core understanding of what it means to follow Jesus. To be a follower of Jesus requires that we submit our lives to the paschal pattern of his life, that is, that we allow life to come from death and personal wholeness to emerge from self-transcendence. Scripture scholars regard Mark 8:22—10:52 as a literary unit, because it is bound together by what is called a "semitic inclusion," a writing technique for weaving seemingly disparate passages into a thematic whole. This "way section" begins with the curing of a blind person at Bethsaida in chapter eight and ends with the healing of the blind beggar Bartimaeus in chapter ten. The two healing incidents serve like bookends providing coherence to the enclosed text. The unifying theme of this section is highlighted by the word "*o odos,*" meaning "the way" or "the road," which appears a total of seven times. According to St. Mark, a Christian disciple is called to follow Jesus "along the way." But this is a slow process of recognizing that our tendency toward selfishness, control, ambition, and competition, and our desire to be the first and the greatest, can stand in the way of loving like Jesus. Mark also tells us that Jesus' disciples were dazed, confused, and unable to see clearly the path laid out by their teacher. Ironically, it is the blind Bartimaeus, not the sighted disciples, who sees most clearly the way of Jesus and thus is able to pursue the Christian path.

WHOLENESS AND HOLINESS CONVERGE IN CONSCIOUS LOVE

Both the "way section" of Mark's gospel and the exhortation to imitate God's love in Matthew's gospel (5:45-46) make clear that the Christian "way" consists in loving. Throughout the New Testament, we are reminded that Jesus' love mirrored God's all-embracing love, because Jesus died for us all. We are called to be like Jesus, who was willing to lay down his life so that others could have life in abundance. Jesus' message to the uncomprehending disciples and to us is that holiness consists in loving others in the context of our daily lives with insight and sensitivity. In the process of striving to love as Jesus did, God will make us whole. Wholeness, for Christians, is not to be sought so much in itself but will result as a kind of by-product of our earnest struggles to love. The spiritual journey entails moving from unconscious to conscious loving.

The cliché "love is blind" captures succinctly what is obviously true about the star-struck infatuation that fuels romantic love. Blind, too, is the "first fervor" of religious neophytes zealously starting on the spiritual path or the heady enthusiasm of young idealists at the beginning of an exciting new project. But a love or commitment that will last cannot remain blind. To endure, it must sooner or later come to see. A love that is faithful throughout a lifetime, persevering over the long haul—whether in marriage, friendship, or celibate commitment—is one that has been given sight. And it is this sight—or, better, "in-sight"—that makes possible love's movement beyond disappointment and disillusionment to choice and commitment. "In-sight" allows love to endure even when it stumbles upon the inevitable hardships that line its path. Growth in consciousness enables us—like the blind Bartimaeus—to follow Jesus faithfully in discipleship. To engage actively in this coming-to-see process, this movement from blind to conscious love, is critical to Christian spiritual growth.

A HOLINESS SOUGHT IN ORDINARY LIFE

While the goal of loving like Jesus is quite lofty, it is meant to take place at home—that is, in the familiar places where we find ourselves and where opportunities to embody the love of Jesus abound. Spiritual growth is achieved through our efforts to love and care in daily ways as husbands and wives, parents and siblings, friends and neighbors, employers and colleagues. Our present lives—just as we find them—are the place where transforming grace is at work making us holy by inspiring us to love like Jesus.

Many ordinary people, without even realizing it, are already following a spiritual path when they strive to love in a self-transcending way. For instance, when the husband of a struggling alcoholic refuses to abandon his wife, yet insists with "tough love" that she be responsible, he is living out gospel love. Or when a wife, instead of condemning her husband for marital infidelity, stays open to the painful process of reconciliation, she is imitating Jesus who said to the woman caught in adultery: "Has no one condemned you? Neither will I." And when parents offer a hospitable and understanding space in which their troubled teenager can weather the storms of growing up, they are embodying the compassion of Jesus. Christian spirituality invites us to deepen our appreciation of the sacredness of ordinary life and to see that our regular routine of work and family life contains countless opportunities for spiritual transformation through self-transcendence.

The Second Vatican Council emphasized the universal call to holiness. Most Christians, however, are still not comfortable with this idea, because their image of being holy is so esoteric that they cannot relate it to their own lives. A story about St. Anthony of Egypt illustrates how sainthood is meant for people of all walks of life.

Once upon a time, more than seventeen hundred years ago, a young man decided to become a saint. He left his home, family and possessions. He said goodbye to relatives and friends, sold all he owned, gave the money to the poor, and walked off into the desert to find God.

He walked through the desert sands until he found a dark cave. "Here," he thought, "I will be alone with God. Here nothing can distract me from God." He prayed day and night in the dark cave. But God sent him great temptations. He imagined all the good things of life and wanted them desperately. However, he was determined to give up everything in order to have God alone. After many months the temptations stopped. St. Anthony of Egypt was at peace, having nothing but God.

But then, according to legend, God said, "Leave your cave for a few days and go off to a distant town. Look for the town shoe-maker. Knock on his door and stay with him for a while."

The holy hermit was puzzled by God's command, but left the next morning. He walked all day across the desert sands. By nightfall he came to the village, found the home of the shoemaker and knocked on the door. A smiling man opened it.

"Are you the town shoemaker?" the hermit asked.

"Yes, I am," the shoemaker answered. He noticed how tired and hungry the hermit looked. "Come in," he said. "You need something to eat and a place to rest." The shoemaker called his wife. They prepared a fine meal for the hermit and gave him a good bed to sleep on.

The hermit stayed with the shoemaker and his family for three days. The hermit asked many questions about their lives. But he didn't tell them much about himself even though the couple were very curious about his life in the desert. They talked a lot and became good friends.

Then the hermit said goodbye to the shoemaker and his wife. He walked back to his cave wondering why God had sent him to visit the shoemaker.

"What was the shoemaker like?" God asked the hermit when he settled down again in his dark cave.

"He is a simple man," the hermit began. "He has a wife who is going to have a baby. They seem to love each other very much. He has a small shop where he makes shoes. He works hard. They have a simple house. They give money and food to those who have less than they have. He and his wife believe very strongly in you and pray at least once a day. They have many friends. And the shoemaker enjoys telling jokes."

God listened carefully. "You are a great saint, Anthony," God said, "and the shoemaker and his wife are great saints, too."[4]

There is a tendency among Christians to shrug off the call to holiness by idealizing the process and seeing it as something that happens to extraordinary people in extraordinary circumstances. Holiness happens, for example, to people who are boiled in hot oil, crucified upside down on the cross, fed to lions because of fidelity to their faith, or murdered at midnight by a right-wing death squad. Traditional images of plastic saints reinforce the tendency to view holiness as something exclusively suited for rare individuals. Thomas Merton describes graphically such a rarified view of sanctity. "The saint, if he ever sinned at all," he states, "eventually became impeccable after a perfect conversion. Impeccability not being quite enough, he is raised beyond the faintest possibility of feeling temptation." Temptation never proves difficult for such holy people because they have the absolute answer and heroic response to it: they fling themselves "into fire, ice water or briers rather than face a remote occasion of sin." They rush, always with the noblest of intentions, to perform the precise act of virtue required by each situation. Seeming somehow to possess certitude about concerns that perplex lesser mortals, "the 'perfect' in this fearsome sense," concludes Merton, "are elevated above the necessity of or even the capacity for a fully human dialogue" with their fellow human beings.[5]

Because Merton's caricature reflects the image of saintliness in the popular imagination, it is not hard to understand why contemporary men and women may regard holiness as something unattainable. Nor is it an attractive goal, because "when the ideal of holiness represents the sum of all virtues," observes religious psychologist Josef Goldbrunner, "a lifeless plaster image is set up and the striving for holiness becomes mere imitation."[6] The criteria set up for determining holiness are often arbitrary, if not asinine, as the following rabbinic story suggests:

> A student of the Torah came to his teacher and announced that, in his opinion, he was qualified for ordination as a rabbi. "What are your qualifications?" asked the sage.
>
> The student replied, "I have disciplined my body so that I can sleep on the ground, eat the grass of the field, and allow myself to be whipped three times a day."
>
> "See that yonder white ass," said the teacher, "and be mindful that it sleeps on the ground, eats the grass of the field, and is whipped no less than three times daily. Up to the present you may qualify to be an ass, but certainly not a rabbi."[7]

Modern images of holiness also feature human giants: Mother Teresa, whose whole life is consumed by care for the poor; Dietrich Bonhoeffer, whose life story is one of the great epics of courage and conviction in our century; Maximilian Kolbe, a priest who offered his life in a Nazi concentration camp in place of a married man who had a wife and children. While we admire these people, their acts of heroic virtue seem beyond our reach, and we find ourselves in search of contemporary models of holiness who are ordinary Christians like ourselves. Unconsciously, we may even disown our own call to holiness by projecting it onto those with an extra-ordinary call. Thus, it is important to claim our vocation to holiness and to view our lives as a process in which God is transforming us in "ordinary" ways. Holiness, like wholeness, is ultimately not of our making but of God's. Yet the call to wholeness and holiness is issued to each of us and requires that we prayerfully consider at all times what following the way of Jesus entails.

THE WAY OF JESUS AND ONE'S PERSONAL PATH

To follow Jesus along the way that leads to holiness requires that each of us discover our personal path and pursue it faithfully. While being recommissioned by the risen Jesus at the Sea of Tiberias after his triple affirmation of love, Peter is momentarily distracted at the sight of John the beloved disciple following them and asks Jesus, "What about him, Lord?" Jesus' response in effect was: "Peter, this is the path I have set for you. Never mind about John. If I want him to stay behind till I come, what does it matter to you? You are to follow me" (Jn 21:20-23). Throughout his life, Jesus modeled what he consistently taught to be the essence of discipleship: a deep resolve to do God's will, a receptivity to the Spirit of God directing one's movements, and an abiding trust that the ever-faithful God will always bring life from death, good from evil. His faith in God enabled him to pursue his particular path even in the face of persecution and powerlessness, rejection and betrayal.

To imitate Christ today is to follow the movements of God as they unfold in the unique and particular pattern that shapes our personal path. As Goldbrunner, applying depth psychology to spiritual development, rightly asserts, "There is no universal way to perfection," but each must find his or her individual way. "The real starting point should be the individual. Authentic sanctity is always bound up with the *uniqueness*, with the limited talents and potentialities of the individual," which are his or her truth. "It is wrong to say: 'That is how I want to develop!' What one should say is: 'What does God expect from me and my particular talents?'"[8] The guiding voice of God may be mysteriously indistinct or inaudible at times. Yet the religious person perseveres in faith, for one "who follows God moves into mystery without prematurely forcing clarity because [one's] experience of God directs this movement."[9]

Fidelity to the path by which we are uniquely called to love in the world requires the same kind of inner freedom and courage that Jesus exhibited when he, despite ridicule and rejection, followed [one's] vision. A common obstacle for many of us who feel inspired to follow Jesus' resoluteness is human respect, the fear of what others are going to think of us. Freedom is gained when the need for human respect is defeated, as the following delightful story illustrates:

> The Master seemed quite impervious to what people thought of him. When the disciples asked how he had attained this stage of inner freedom, he laughed aloud and said, "Till I was twenty I did not care what people thought of me. After twenty I worried endlessly about what my neighbors thought. Then one day after fifty I suddenly saw that they hardly ever thought of me at all!"[10]

Genuine imitation of Christ consists in following his example of deep devotion to God and unwavering pursuit of his vision of proclaiming the kingdom, rather than simply imitating the external aspects of his life. Mere mindless imitation will get us nowhere on the spiritual path.

> After the Master attained Enlightenment, he took to living simply—because he found simple living to his taste.

> He laughed at his disciples when they took to simple living in imitation of him.

> "Of what use is it to copy my behavior," he would say, "without my motivation? Or to adopt my motivation without the vision that produced it?"

> They understood him better when he said, "Does a goat become a rabbi because he grows a beard?"[11]

Like Jesus, we too must, through prayer and reflection, stay in touch with our inner call and the Spirit-inspired vision for our lives.

THE PROCESS OF INDIVIDUATION

Put in the language of Jungian psychology, pursuing our personal path involves individuation, the process by which we become ourselves, indivisible and distinct from other people. We grow in wholeness by becoming conscious of "the shadow," Jung's term for those parts of ourselves that are buried in the unconscious. We become distinct from other people by affirming our uniqueness as individuals. Psychologist Lawrence Jaffe comments that many of his clients are "often possessed by the uncontrollable desire to be what they call normal, by which they generally mean just like everyone else. They forget they were meant to be something unprecedented...a mystery that only they, with the help of God, can realize by living their life...with the sincerity and devotion that Christ lived his."[12]

Biblical spirituality describes individuation as the ongoing process of being reunited with something that has been lost. This is clearly seen in chapter fifteen, the so-called "lost and found department" of Luke's gospel, in which a coin, a sheep, and a child are lost and then found. In the well-known parable of the lost son, Jesus invites us to claim the part of us that is prodigal like the younger son, as well as the part of us that is righteous like the elder son. The good news of the parable is that God is one who embraces with love and acceptance all the parts that make up ourselves. Conversion of heart requires that we extend to ourselves the same kind of acceptance that God so readily gives to us. This means accepting the peculiar amalgam of strengths and weaknesses that we find ourselves to be and pursuing our own destiny without giving in to human respect and the need "to be normal."

In the life of Jesus, the path of individuation was a "way of the cross." And so it is for us. Our way of the cross today lies in the abandonment of perfectionistic striving, embracing instead a spirituality of wholeness or integration. Episcopal priest and Jungian analyst John Sanford reminds us that "becoming whole does not mean being perfect, but being complete. It does not necessarily mean happiness, but growth. It is often painful, but never boring."[13]

CONFRONTING THE UNCONSCIOUS

Spiritual writers and psychologists have used the term "false self" to suggest how untruthful our self-image can be when aspects of the self are denied and repressed. The journey toward wholeness necessitates getting to know our shadow and confronting our unknown motivations and attitudes. Because this requires going deeper into ourselves, images of descent rather than ascent seem more descriptive of this aspect of the spiritual journey. Thus, terms such as "going deeper," "soul-searching" and "uncovering" more closely capture what the spiritual journey involves.

In his ongoing polemic against the traditions of the Pharisees, Jesus consistently insists on the need to go beyond mere reliance on externals and superficial observance of the Law. For Jesus, what clearly counts in terms of spiritual transformation is not externals, but the interior dispositions of one's *kardia*, or heart. The word *kardia* is used in the New Testament to symbolize our innermost feelings, emotions, and judgments. To grow spiritually, we must go below the surface of neat appearance and proper behavior and examine our hearts, "for it is from within, from the heart [*kardia*], that evil intentions emerge: fornication, theft, murder, adultery, avarice, malice, deceit, indecency, envy, slander, pride, folly. All these evil things come from within and make a person unclean" (Mk 7:21-22). "But eating with unwashed hands does not make anyone unclean" (Mt 15:20). Thus, the teaching of Jesus is quite clear: it is the human heart that needs to be purified, so that God's Spirit can transform us into a new creation. The wisdom of Solomon lay in his intuition that "an understanding heart" was the most precious of gifts that he could request of God. What Solomon received from God is what we need also to seek in our spiritual journey. We need hearts that understand what lies in our inner depths.

Recognizing the importance of self-knowledge and inner work for spiritual growth, Cistercian abbot Thomas Keating reaffirms the wisdom of depth psychology: "The heart of the Christian ascesis is the struggle with our unconscious motivations. If we do not recognize and confront the hidden influences of the emotional programs for happiness, the false self will adjust to any new situation in a short time and nothing is really changed."[14] This means that if we are serious about growing spiritually, we will have to deal with our shadow, something we initially resist because it goes against the grain; or, as Jung put it, is *contra naturam*, contrary to our nature. But eventually we may be pressed by necessity to do what we otherwise would not. While things are going along smoothly, we are content to live with superficial consciousness. However, when suffering disturbs our lives, upsetting our equilibrium and "throwing us for a loop," we become motivated to do some serious soul-searching. Events such as the sudden death of a loved one, a failed relationship, or the onset of a debilitating disease force us to discover anew that which will sustain us. Depression, chronic anxiety, and various forms of physical illness and addictions are also ways in which the psyche can express unconscious conflicts and signal the need for honest self-confrontation. Such suffering can serve as a gateway to further growth by nudging us into places we would otherwise not go.

DEALING WITH OUR AMBIVALENCE

Commitment to growth in consciousness and wholeness exacts a price and those drawn to such a commitment naturally experience ambivalence and resistance. The encounter of Jesus with the paralytic at the pool of Bethesda (Jn 5:1-9) points out the need for deliberation before we commit ourselves to such a transforming process. Of the sick man, stranded and immobile at the side of the pool for thirty-eight years, Jesus asked, "Do you want to be healed?" This question does not seem initially to make sense. It would seem obvious that anyone stuck in such a paralyzed place would desperately want to be cured. Upon reflection, however, Jesus' question had a purpose. It invited the paralytic to carefully consider how a cure would drastically alter his life and whether he would be willing to embrace these changes. Was he willing to abandon a familiar routine, constrained and limited though it was, to risk a radically new way of living? It is not uncommon to hear doctors and other health professionals talk about the unconscious resistance they encounter with patients who, in fact, do not want to become well because they fear the concrete changes they would have to make in their life and relationships.

Similarly, the question "Do you want to be more conscious, more whole?" acknowledges that a "yes" to such growth will bring us new challenges. Self-confrontation is a painful, but necessary, part of psychological and spiritual growth. "Pain is one of the sure signs that contemplation is happening," states a contemporary spiritual writer. While contemplation may lead eventually to bliss, "first it gives us the pain of knowing that some of our dearest convictions are shallow, inadequate, wrong. Contemplation first deprives us of familiar comforts. Then it replaces them with an inner emptiness in which new truth, often alien and unsettling truth, can emerge."[15]

Christian tradition has always seen the connection between spiritual growth and painful purification. Witness the desert fathers and mothers who wrestled with their demons, and cloistered contemplatives, like John of the Cross, who struggled with the dark night of the soul. Some contemporary spiritual writers believe that psychology is a necessary tool to understanding such spiritual experiences as those described by St. John of the Cross. Not only is its language more familiar to our western ears than the language of traditional spiritual theology, but psychology also explains how nature and grace must cooperate in the process of transformation and healing.[16]

The inevitable struggles entailed in living like Christ gain significance when they are viewed as the mystery of God's purifying action in our lives. While not every experience of unsought pain and darkness counts as a mystical "dark night" by which God brings about greater union with us, "many (perhaps most or all) negative experiences," claims a contemporary Carmelite scholar, "have the potential to *become* elements in, or concrete incarnations of, the 'passive nights,' when confronted in faith, hope, and love."[17] The purifying "passive nights" described by John of the Cross are experienced by most Christians today "not within the security of a traditional monastic cell, but more often in 'suffering for a cause,' or in the purification of one's ministerial commitments through failure and disillusionment, or even in 'the quiet martyrdom of everyday life.'"[18] Dag Hammarskjöld and Dorothy Day, for example, were made holy through their lifelong fidelity to an inner call. Thus, the sufferings experienced in daily living can contribute to our spiritual growth. Like the branch that is pruned so that it can bear more abundant fruit, we may also discover in our frustrations and pain the transforming action of God in our lives.

"DROP YOUR NETS INTO THE DEEP"

Luke's narrative of the call of the first disciples (5:1-9) graphically conveys God's invitation to go deeper and the reassurance that anything we discover within ourselves can be transformed by God's grace. After a frustrating night of fruitless toil, Peter and his companions are cleaning their nets in preparation for quitting work. Suddenly, Jesus appears on the bank, just off shore, teaching the crowd. As the crowd pushes in on him, Jesus gets into Peter's boat and asks him to pull out a little from the shore. Then Jesus directs Peter to "put out into deep water and pay out your nets for a catch." Jesus' request is met initially by Peter's resistance: "Master, we worked hard all night long and caught nothing." But Peter eventually relents: "...but if you say so, I will pay out the nets." They then catch such a huge number of fish that their nets begin to tear. They call their companions to come help with a second boat and the final catch fills both boats nearly to the sinking point.

Jesus' invitation to drop our nets into the deep can be seen as an invitation to self-knowledge and interiority. Peter's initial resistance reflects the same reluctance and fear that we experience when we are called to leave the surface and go to another level of our being. We worry about what we might encounter in the depths of our soul. We wonder whether the gain is worth the effort and possible pain. Like the fearful Peter who fell at the knees of Jesus after the miraculous catch of fish saying, "Leave me, Lord; I am a sinful person," our resisting and fearful selves also need to hear Jesus' reassuring words: "Do not be afraid; from now on it is people you will catch." In this reassurance, we can hear the risen Jesus say to us: "Do not be afraid. I will be with you. Anything you dredge up from the depth of your being I will use for good." So we contemporary disciples are likewise reassured that as we grow in self-knowledge and wholeness, our greater fullness as human beings will allow God to bring about a huge catch that will nourish ourselves as well as others.

Using another gospel image, Christian spirituality can be envisioned as a journey through the field of the self to discover a buried treasure within. The treasure is the indwelling presence of God. As Christ put it, "The kingdom of heaven is like a treasure hidden in a field which someone has found; the person hides it again, goes off happily, sells everything...and buys the field" (Mt 13:44). This inner journey entails a trek through the psyche's many layers of consciousness. It is frightening when we face unknown terrain. This journey, states Jesuit author Gerald Hughes, "will always be accompanied by some measure of uncertainty, pain, and confusion. These negative feelings are the nudgings of God."[19] Trusting in God's sustaining love can keep us on the path; following Jesus' invitation to go deeper can bring us to an amazing discovery of the kingdom within. It is in light of this that Teilhard de Chardin, the priest, scientist, and mystic, exhorted: "Let us leave the surface, and without leaving the world, plunge into God."

Reflection Questions

1. Have you ever identified with St. Paul's struggle with the divided self? How do you experience fragmentation in your life? In what areas of your life do you hunger for wholeness?

2. What have been some spiritual practices you have tried in order to achieve wholeness, balance, and harmony in your life? What has worked for you? What has not?

3. Jesus' invitation to Peter to "drop the nets into the deep" can symbolize a similar invitation given to all of us to drop below the surface and to live with more depth, consciousness, and meaning. If you were to respond to this invitation, what would it entail in the concrete way in which you live your daily life? What in you may resist this invitation to "go deeper"?

CHAPTER TWO

THE ABANDONED SELF:
THE SHADOW AND WHOLENESS

...there is no light without shadow and no psychic wholeness without
imperfection. To round itself out, life calls not for perfection but for
completeness; and for this the 'thorn in the flesh' is needed, the suffering of
defects without which there is no progress and no ascent.[1]
—C. G. Jung
DREAMS

IN HER CLASSIC work *The Interior Castle*, St. Teresa images the soul as a
mansion with many rooms and suggests that spiritual growth
involves the ability to move freely from one room to another without
fear or inhibition. There is, she says, one room in which we should
always live, and that is the room of self-knowledge. For Teresa, self-
knowledge is the sine qua non of holiness because self-knowledge
leads to humility. "Self-knowledge is the traditional term," Cistercian
abbot Thomas Keating reminds us, "for the coming to consciousness
of the dark side of one's personality."[2] While Teresa did not use such
terms as "consciousness," "shadow," or "inner life," her message is
clear: becoming aware of one's inner life is the cornerstone of both
spiritual and psychological growth. Carl Jung, who explored the
depths of the human psyche, discovered that self-knowledge is so
important to the health of the soul that it should be considered a
religious undertaking. In his psychology, getting to know the shadow,
"the thing a person has no wish to be," is a way of redeeming all the
rejected and lost parts of the soul.

WHAT IS THE SHADOW?

Jung used the term "shadow" to describe the part of our personality that we repress because it conflicts with the way we wish to see ourselves. If aspects of ourselves like sexuality, anger, ambition, or creativity, for example, do not fit our desired self-image, they will be relegated to the shadow. The shadow is an inferior subpersonality that has its own life, with goals and values that contradict those we consciously hold. There is a saying that "the brighter the persona, the darker the shadow." In contrast to the shadow, which is the face we hide, the persona is the public self, the face we show to the outer world. The more we identify with an overly good or righteous persona, the darker will be our shadow. When there is too big a gap between our "wishful" image and our true self, we will be constantly troubled by anxiety because we fear that others will see through us.

Although the shadow has a sinister and guilt-ridden quality, Jung never intended the shadow to get the bad reputation it has. The shadow only seems "bad" because it houses all the unacceptable and inferior parts of us. If anything, Jung saw the shadow more as a treasure hidden in a field, a potential source of richness that is unavailable to us as long as it is buried. We need to rethink our attitude toward the shadow, "that which we have no wish to be," because it contains that which will make us whole.

HOW THE SHADOW IS FORMED

The shadow is the opposite side of our conscious personality. Each of us possesses an ideal self, a picture of the kind of person we think we should be. This idealistic image is largely formed by our early experiences of family and culture. As young children we were taught certain values and were judged "good" when we conformed to them and "bad" when we did not. We learned to hide or repress whatever parts of ourselves brought adult disapproval and punishment. The poet-philosopher Robert Bly gives a personal account of how the shadow develops.

> When we were one or two years old we had what we might visualize as a 360-degree personality. Energy radiated out from all parts of our body and all parts of our psyche. A child running is a living

globe of energy. We had a ball of energy, all right; but one day we noticed that our parents didn't like certain parts of that ball. They said things like: "Can't you be still?" Or "It isn't nice to try and kill your brother." Behind us we have an invisible bag, and the part of us our parents don't like, we, to keep our parents' love, put in the bag. By the time we go to school our bag is quite large. Then our teachers have their say: "Good children don't get angry over such little things." So we take our anger and put it in the bag. By the time my brother and I were twelve in Madison, Minnesota, we were known as "the nice Bly boys." Our bags were already a mile long.[3]

Bly goes on to describe how this bag stuffing continues as we move beyond our family of origin into other groups, where we find that new expectations await us. For example, we join a sorority or fraternity and anxiously mold our behavior in order to belong. Or we get married, and we must accommodate our in-laws for the sake of pleasing our spouse. We join a religious community and find ourselves in a distinct subculture that must become our own. Or we transfer from one office to another within the same company and discover that here a different set of norms governs what is acceptable. Clearly, groups have an idealized image that pressures us to measure up. Our desire for acceptance and approval causes us to monitor ourselves in order to conform to group norms. In the process of these adult experiences, our shadow continues to grow, as more of ourselves are stuffed into the bag. The result is that many of us end up at midlife with only a slice of the 360-degree personality that we began life with. And then we spend the rest of our lives reclaiming what is in the bag!

THE JOURNEY INWARD

Reclaiming what has been lost in the shadow is an essential aspect of the inner journey. As human beings, we are a mixture of darkness and light, good and evil, capable of the best of any saint and the worst of any sinner. We grow in wholeness by becoming aware of and accepting our multidimensional selves. Integrating the shadow requires a lifetime of inner work and is never achieved once and for all. Inner work—the process of knowing, healing, and harmonizing our inner life—is the essence of spirituality because it is our inner life that influences our perceptions, desires, thoughts, and actions.

Ignoring the inner world because we do not like what we find, or postponing inner work out of fear of what we might discover, makes the shadow increasingly difficult to deal with. The energies in the shadow grow more primitive with age, not unlike what happens to a person who is caged in solitary confinement and deprived of all human contact. The longer instincts are repressed, the more hostile they become.

Misconceptions about Inner Work and the Shadow

There are three popular misconceptions that can make us shy away from the kind of inner work required by the spiritual journey. The first is that self-reflection necessarily leads to selfishness and navel-gazing rather than self-giving. This misconception, based on the idea that holiness consists in self-negation and self-abandonment, expresses a kind of dualistic thinking that sees everything in either-or terms: self-centered or other-centered, selfish or generous. A valuable insight that depth psychology offers us on our spiritual journey is that genuine holiness requires both self-awareness *and* self-transformation.

As Christians, we pattern ourselves after Christ, whose gift of self to others was the natural response of a person with a deep sense of being the beloved Son of God. "God so loved the world that [God] gave [God's] own Son," states John's gospel (3:16), and the Son so loved us that he gave himself up so that we might have abundant life. Striving to love as Jesus did and seeking genuine Christian self-transcendence necessitate an ongoing process of examining our motives for giving. Things are not always what they seem. Just as "hook humility" is meant to draw praise, spurious forms of self-transcendence are egocentric. They may appear to be altruistic but in fact have hidden strings attached because they are motivated by unconscious or covert needs for recognition and approval, for security and power. Swiss psychiatrist Alice Miller, for example, has long called our attention to how parents and other caregivers often unconsciously use their children to gratify their covert needs.[4] Self-giving falls far short of the kind of self-transcendence modeled by Jesus, whenever it stems from affective deprivation, low self-esteem, or ulterior motives of profit and gain, and whenever it is compulsively fueled by the need to be needed. Critics who are suspicious of self-reflection, crying "Enough of introspection! Beware of the narcissism that comes with monitoring every twitch of the psyche!" need to realize that inner work is not only for the soul but also for the whole body of Christ. Ongoing self-awareness, assisted by illuminating grace, helps us walk steadily on the path of loving as Jesus did and alerts us to unconscious self-seeking camouflaged as Christian service. "In contrast to some other traditions," states Benedictine monk Brother David Steindl-Rast, "Christians have not done particularly well in cultivating a practical method for integrating the shadow. This is part of the reason we have some of the problems that plague us today."[5]

The second misconception, based on a distorted understanding of Jung, identifies the concept of the shadow with the Christian notion of sin. Whereas sin represents rejection of God, the shadow represents rejection of self. Sin is spiritual alienation and requires reconciliation with God. The shadow represents self-alienation and requires reconciliation with the self. If we hate the shadow as we hate sin, we will always remain divided. The shadow becomes a problem only when we mistakenly transfer our negative attitudes toward sin onto the shadow. The appropriate religious attitude toward sin is to rid it from our lives. When we take this dismissive attitude toward the shadow, we jeopardize our development into wholeness and perpetuate our self-alienation. If the shadow were merely evil, there would be no ambiguity in how to deal with it. But, as Jung makes clear, "The unconscious is not just evil by nature, it is also the source of the highest good: not only dark, but also light; not only bestial, semi-human and demonic, but superhuman, spiritual, and, in the classical sense of the word, 'divine.'"[6]

The third misconception has to do with the confusion between "integrating" and "acting out" the shadow. People commonly fear that if they get in touch with their shadow, they will act it out. For example, we may fear that admitting our sexual impulses and desires will lead to living them out in inappropriate ways. But the contrary is true. Acting out stems from unconsciousness. Consciousness gives us choice and makes us able to respond in a deliberate way, according to our moral and ethical principles. It is when we split off from our instincts that we are most in danger of acting them out. The aim of consciousness is self-discovery and personal responsibility. The more we know about our own human instincts and desires, the more responsibly we can live.

GOOD PEOPLE'S STRUGGLE WITH THE SHADOW

Religious people are particularly vulnerable to difficult shadow problems because we set our sights so high, consciously striving to be good and virtuous. There is a psychological law that says that the more we consciously strive for some good, the more its dark opposite will be activated. If, for example, our conscious ego ideal is to be like Christ, then our shadow will contain all our un-Christlike features. And the more we think that we are like Christ, the less likely we are to see our shadow. And because whatever is in the unconscious gets projected, we will simultaneously project our shadow onto others and feel compelled to correct or "help" them. Meanwhile, we neglect our real need to confront the shadow in ourselves. Such shadow projection easily breeds fanaticism, as in the case of antipornography crusaders, who cannot own up to their own prurient fixation on sex, or homophobic gay-bashers, who are fearfully intolerant of the slightest trace of homosexual feeling in themselves.

If we equate holiness with perfection, we will find it impossible to recognize our shadow. To try to live as if we were pure light, devoid of any darkness, is not only pretentious but dangerous. The shadow aspect of our lives can be projected, denied, or ignored, but it cannot be obliterated. The more it is repressed, the more it leads its own life. Denial of the shadow allows it to act on its own, without the benefit of conscious control and guidance. The pharisaic tendency to equate holiness with perfect observance leaves one vulnerable to shadow eruptions, because denial of the shadow is like giving an untamed horse its own rein. A one-sided identification with light, for example, has allowed the disowned shadow to bring about the painful downfall of more than a few religious leaders.

The autonomous nature of the shadow is apparent in the "scandals" that have proliferated in the media in recent years. Religious leaders who have lived in the public light, rigorously attempting to carry the projection of light for their followers, have been exposed as other than what they have projected. Shadow seepage is also evidenced in the growing pile of statistics that reveal sexual abuse performed "in the name of God," supposedly upholding impossibly rigid and perfectionistic family rules, while the darkness of night shrouds the secrecy of traumatic exploitation.[7]

How much easier it is to spot evil in others while being blind to the very same evil in ourselves. The Old Testament story of the prophet Nathan's rebuke of the great King David, bringing him to repentance (2 Sam 12:1-15), is a graphic illustration of this. Nathan came to David and said:

> In the same town were two men, one rich and one poor. The rich man had flocks and herds in great abundance; the poor man had nothing but a ewe lamb, only a single little one which he had bought. He fostered it and it grew up with him and his children, eating his bread, drinking from his cup, sleeping in his arms; it was like a daughter to him. When a traveller came to stay, the rich man would not take anything from his own flock or herd to provide for the wayfarer who had come to him. Instead, he stole the poor man's lamb and prepared that for his guest.

When he heard this story, David was deeply enraged and said to Nathan, "The man who did this deserves to die. For doing such a thing and for having shown no pity, he shall make fourfold restitution for the lamb." In response, Nathan said to David, "You are the man!" Through the use of a story, the shrewd prophet was able to jar the king's conscience and make him aware of the horrible evil he had perpetrated on a man named Uriah the Hittite. Already having many wives, David took Uriah's wife Bathsheba and added her to his harem. Moreover, with cunning calculation he set Uriah up to be killed in battle. The prophet's directness brought the king's shadow out of the dark cave of unconsciousness and allowed him to confess his evil deed: "I have sinned against Yahweh!" David's humble admission of his sin has always been regarded as one of the main reasons why he is so revered and honored in the Judeo-Christian tradition.

In the New Testament, Jesus reminds us that it is easier to spot the faults of others than to recognize our own. The speck we see in our neighbor's eye mirrors the log in our own. The teaching of Jesus is clear: whenever we are tempted to correct someone else, we should look first for that fault in ourselves. In his ongoing debate with the Pharisees, Jesus consistently points to the need for confronting our own shadow if we are to be saved. The Pharisees symbolize those who identify with their persona of righteousness and do not acknowledge their dark side. In their self-righteousness, they feel no need for receiving salvation from a God who is forgiving and accepting. Those who know their shadow, on the other hand, openly acknowledge their need for transforming grace as they struggle to love and accept themselves and others as Jesus did. Pharisaic self-righteousness not only blocks our path to God, it also robs us of compassion and solidarity with others who suffer. When we realize that St. Augustine's "There but for the grace of God go I" expresses a truth about us all, we will be slower to condemn and quicker to forgive.

INTEGRATING THE SHADOW

The shadow manifests itself in a variety of ways in our everyday lives. The story of how a person stumbled into his own "shadow face" in a hostile confrontation with a neighbor who lived down the road provides a concrete illustration.

Down the road from where I live, lives my shadow.

It is amazing that such a powerful thing could escape my notice, but there it is. I have lived most of my life in relative ignorance of this powerful force, assuming (as most of us do) that what I see on the surface is all that is true, and that what I see in others has nothing to do with me.

The story of my shadow that lives down the road is a story of rude awakening—an awakening into a realm of meaning that was inaccessible to my surface consciousness, and yet was always there, waiting for me.

My house stands at the top of a mountain, with a single access road about three miles long. I drive a red sports car and I am often in a hurry to get up or down this long road to my house.

On this particular day, I was driving in my usual manner—fast—when I heard a shout. Actually, it was more of a roar. Even over the stereo and the road noise, I could make out the words: "Slow down!"

I was startled out of my reverie and a number of thoughts and feelings began to flash through me. I was thrown into a state of powerful reactivity. Who had the audacity to say such a thing to me, to tell *me* how to drive, to interfere with *my* right to do exactly what I feel like doing?

I could feel my anger rising, a survival/rage reflex coming up fast and hard. I was incensed, seeing red, blinded with it. Who *dares*?

I braked hard into a long slide and a flurry of dust on the

unpaved road. I stepped out of my car, a challenge in my heart and my voice: "Excuse me?" I said, with thinly veiled hostility.

The answer was quickly forthcoming. A stream of profanity issued forth from somewhere and I gradually located its source above me: a large and very angry man, whom I vaguely recognized as one of my neighbors, had obviously taken more than mild offense at my driving habits. He let loose a torrent of obscenity and accusation that was completely unexpected and overpowering in its violence. He proceeded to curse me with every known profanity, swearing at a bellow that he would kill me, and anyone who even resembled me, but not without eviscerating me first with his bare hands. The litany of curses and threats continued, his raging voice a broad, clear channel to the root of the human violence.

The unexpected power of his response shifted my consciousness immediately and profoundly. As I stood in the stream of fury, unable to understand how I had unleashed this awesome blast of rage, I had a sudden realization—I immediately understood that this explosion of temper was my *own*. It was the astonishing power and depth of my own anger reflected back to me. With this sudden and total shift came the clear understanding that I was looking at myself, into the depths of my own murderous rage. I instantly understood that there was no difference between us—that his anger outside, and my anger inside, were the same. All my feelings of reactivity, of defense, of indignation were gone, replaced in a moment with the certain knowledge that I was looking into the face of my own anger—my own *shadow face*.

I saw at once that this shadow quality, which I ordinarily kept hidden from myself, was actually a crucial component of my own psyche, a rich and dangerous vitality that was bottled up underneath my acceptable personality. It was the well of my own life blood that exploded forth in that moment. I saw that, far from being something that I could disown, this level of rage was actually well within my range. Indeed, this awesome, overwhelming rage was my own life energy, bottled up and hidden until it burst through in this peak event, this rude awakening.[8]

To begin to process everyday events such as this in a psychologically fruitful way requires an understanding that there is more to ourselves and our world than we typically assume. The narrator of this vivid account admits that this event which precipitated the discovery of his shadow, like that of other ordinary occurrences of daily life, could have been understood on a more superficial level. He could have dismissed the experience as merely an unfortunate run-in with someone with an obvious problem with pent-up rage, and thereby learned nothing about himself. Learning to recognize our shadow when it appears is an invaluable means for growth in self-knowledge. The more we can open ourselves to see the truth of who we are, the more whole we can become: "The ability to see my own reflection in the face of my enraged neighbor flooded my awareness with information about myself that I had never accessed in such a direct and dynamic way. It was a moment of healing, of remembering a part of myself that had been lost and forgotten, and in that way was a leap toward wholeness."[9]

Our projections transform the world around us into a mirror that shows us our own faces, although we do not recognize them as our own. These projections so form our attitudes toward others that eventually we bring about what we project. If we project negative intentions onto others, we will react to them with anger and defensiveness. Others will experience our unprovoked hostility and this will arouse their defensiveness and negative shadow projections, which in turn will make us more defensive, and thus bad feelings escalate. Only when we begin to recognize and integrate the shadow will such an impasse end. Knowing how the shadow speaks to us will give us the ability to recognize it. Here are some helpful ways to identify the shadow.

Projection. By Jung's definition, a man's shadow is masculine and a woman's is feminine. Projection of the shadow, then, is usually onto a person of the same sex. While it is possible to project the shadow onto the opposite sex, we tend to accept our shadow when we see it in the opposite sex. For example, a woman may like "strong" men but reject "strong" women; a man may be drawn to women who are passive but regard such men as weak. The way we know that another person is personifying our shadow is by the intensity of our emotional reaction to that person. When we have a strong positive or negative reaction to someone, that person is likely to be carrying an aspect of our shadow. People whom we fiercely criticize, whom we cannot stand to be around, who irritate and upset us, whom we consider to be our enemy, may be carrying aspects of ourselves that we detest. Or, alternatively, those whom we admire and idealize may carry positive qualities and traits of ours that we are blind to. We can tell that a piece of our own shadow has been projected onto our neighbor when we feel a strong urge or compulsion to criticize or sanctify his or her behavior.

The question is often asked about the difference between projection and perception. When, for example, are we reacting to a negative trait that really exists in another and when are we projecting a disowned part of ourselves onto that person? When projection is involved, we react disproportionately to what we perceive because our response is influenced by an unconscious agenda. When, however, our reactions are mild, that is, we see something in another that we dislike, but do not feel unduly excited about it, we are probably not projecting, but merely noticing what is objectively there. For example, if we see someone behaving selfishly and have repressed our own selfish tendencies so that we regard ourselves as never selfish, then we will feel much more judgmental toward that person than we would if we had accepted our own selfishness. Our projection causes us to overreact to their selfishness because it saddles them with a double dose of it; they carry ours as well as their own. A projection is like an arrow. It has to hit a porous target in order to stick. Those who attract our projections do so because they possess some quality that is a rejected aspect of ourselves, and we find ourselves "stuck" to them, as an arrow to a target. If it is something we have accepted in ourselves, then we will be more accepting of those who share that similarity with us.

If we want to learn about our shadow, we can begin by noticing our reactions to others. What qualities provoke our self-righteous indignation? What characteristics do we value most highly and find most praiseworthy? Who evokes our judgment? Our admiration? The answers to such questions may lead us to some enlightening and surprising discoveries.

Inner Voice. Besides projection, the shadow sometimes expresses itself as a voice inside us—another self—with whom we dialogue. During times of decision making or inner conflict, that other voice engaging us in an inner debate may be the shadow voicing its desires. To make good decisions, we need the views of this "other." Bad choices or errors in judgment are often the results of not listening to the shadow.

Freudian Slips. The shadow can also be observed in "Freudian slips"—instances when we mean to say one thing but say something else instead. The slip is usually something embarrassing or hostile, something we had no intention of saying. If we honestly examine these mistakes, we might find that they reveal a hidden hurt or anger, some feeling that the shadow has carried for us until it found an opportunity to express it. The shadow gets revenge for the hurts that we repress, and sometimes at our expense.

Humor. If we examine what we say in humor as well as what evokes our laughter we can often detect our shadow. Humor is one of the shadow's hiding places and it reveals much more about us than we think. The lack of a sense of humor is equally telling and usually indicates great rigidity and repression. To illustrate how humor reveals the shadow, psychologist William Miller tells the story of three clergymen in a small town who met each week to support each other:

> The longer they met the more intimate and trusting they became. One day they decided that they had reached the level of trust where each could confess his gravest sin to the others and thus share his guilt. "I confess that I steal money from the offering," said the first. "That *is* bad," said the second, who then went on to confess, "My gravest sin is having an affair with a woman in the adjacent town." The third clergy, hearing the wretchedness of the other two declared, "Oh my brothers, I must confess to you that my most terrible sin is gossip; and I can't wait to get out of here!"[10]

The gossip in us gets a vicarious kick out of this story. We find it funny because we can identify with the third clergyman and imagine the pleasure of spreading such a secret. Our spontaneous laughter allows us to see a part of ourselves and to accept that, no matter how wrong it is to gossip, we too have a gossip in us. On the other hand, if we are in denial about our shadow we are apt to judge, rather than laugh at, the clergyman.

Dreams. Another source of shadow material is given to us each night in the form of dreams. Dreams, the language of the unconscious, are one of the best ways to get to know the shadow because during sleep our defenses are lowered, allowing the unconscious to speak without interference. The known and unknown women in a woman's dream, for instance, reveal to her the various qualities of her shadow personality. Similarly, a man's shadow personality will be personified by the masculine images in his dreams.[11] Aspects of ourselves that are hidden backstage during the day find their way onto center stage in the nocturnal dramas created by our dreams. If we observe these dramas carefully, we will see our shadow played out nightly and learn much about our unspoken motives, hidden faults and failures, unacknowledged virtues and vices, and undeveloped or unrealized potential.

THE SHADOW AND RELATIONSHIPS

Shadow projections influence how we see, feel and respond to others. The shadow is at work behind the scenes in those recurring arguments, conflicts, and power struggles that we have with others. The need always to be right, to have our own way, to dominate and control are indicative of our unconscious shadow motives. The extent of the interpersonal havoc that the shadow can create ranges from the breakup of important relationships (marriages, friendships, communities) to the outbreak of war and genocide. In community or family life, where people live closely together, shadow problems are both inevitable and subtle. The following are some signs that the shadow is at work.

Scapegoating. Scapegoating, the identification and labeling of one person in the group as "the problem," is a well-known phenomenon in the Judeo-Christian heritage and a common problem in contemporary group life. Jesus is often seen as a scapegoat, as are many Old Testament prophets before him. We all have had some experience of scapegoating in either our work or personal lives. Scapegoating is the result of shadow projections. One person becomes the object of the negative shadow projections of the whole group. He or she is "chosen" to carry the blame for what is, in fact, an unacknowledged group need or conflict. The feeling tone is, "If it weren't for that misfit, everything in our group would be fine." This belief can contaminate the designated scapegoat, because when people live or work closely together, their projections or expectations inevitably influence each other, for good or ill. We tend to become what others perceive us to be, because they treat us accordingly. If, for example, someone projects selfishness onto me and punishes me by withholding, I will respond in kind and thus end up acting selfishly. If, on the other hand, the same person projects generosity onto me and rewards me by being generous to me, I will reciprocate with generosity.

Perfectionism. We occasionally come across people who seem to be untouched by original sin and have no shadow. They appear to be "above it all," without noticeable faults or weaknesses, always doing the right thing, consistently generous and kind, never uncharitable toward anyone. We may think that these rare individuals are better than human, "perfect Christians." But perfection is not humanly possible; everyone has faults, even saints. No one is perfectly kind, generous, and charitable all of the time. Where, then, is the shadow in the lives of these "holy innocents"? Most likely, others in the group are carrying it for them. When we, in our need to be perfect, deny our dark side, others are compelled to express those human reactions for us. In other words, when we refuse to carry the cross of our darkness, others get saddled with it.

People who seem "too good to be true" may irritate rather than inspire us. We may intuit that they are not genuine, but rather hiding their true feelings and reactions so that others will admire them. False goodness in others can make us feel inferior because it magnifies our own shortcomings and at times even seems to draw out our own dark side. We might, for example, find ourselves watching and hoping that these seemingly shadowless specimens of virtue will somehow slip up or make a mistake. And when they do, we take secret pleasure in their failure, because now they seem human like the rest of us.

Inferiority. Another type of shadow problem is manifested in an inferiority complex, which results when we project the positive aspects of our personality onto others. In our society, many people suffer from low self-esteem and feelings of inadequacy. Passive and dependent on others, they see themselves as having little to offer and generally feel sorry for themselves. Although they participate in life, they do so from the sidelines because they think that they are not "good enough" to make an individual and creative contribution. This is a shadow problem, but in this case it is not undesirable qualities but rather undeveloped gifts and talents that are repressed and attributed to others. Those who feel inferior do so because they have not found their own niche in life. This failure makes them sensitive to others' achievements. They tend to overvalue the gifts of others, admiring them and wishing to be like them. Instead of fulfilling their own potential and offering what they have, they put those whom they admire on pedestals and expect too much of them. The danger involved in chronic projection of our positive shadow is that it can become an easy escape from the responsibility to develop and use our God-given talents for the service of others.

MORAL SIGNIFICANCE OF THE SHADOW

Dealing with the shadow can become a moral responsibility as well as a necessity for personal growth. It is apparent from the foregoing examples of shadow problems that our repressed shadow can have a destructive influence on others without our knowledge or our conscious intent. Shadow projections occur spontaneously in our relationships with others. We do not deliberately project our shadow qualities onto others; it happens before we know it. How then can we be morally responsible for something that happens without our consent? The important issue here is not that shadow problems exist or that projections occur, but whether or not we choose to get to know our own shadow so that we can recognize when we are projecting it onto others. The realization that we are seeing ourselves reflected in our neighbor enables us to withdraw our projection from those who personify it and then to deal with it in ourselves. If we do this, we can free ourselves of the compulsion to "take the speck out of our neighbor's eye" and can acknowledge the log in our own. If we do not, we force others to carry our dark side for us. Perhaps Jesus had this in mind when he said that being his follower requires the willingness to take up one's own cross. The hardest burden to bear is one's own individual nature and fate. This, however, is the essence of moral integrity and, according to Jung, the cornerstone of a truly religious attitude and way of life.

TOLERANCE FOR AMBIGUITY AND GUILT

Since much of what is in the shadow is guilt-laden, we can expect that we will experience guilt feelings when we notice our shadow. Guilt does not always indicate that we are doing something morally wrong or sinful. More often than we realize, our feelings of guilt stem from going against ways of thinking, feeling, and behaving that we have associated with the right and proper way of being. For example, when people accustomed to swallowing their anger begin to take notice and express it, they may feel a twinge of guilt. Or when recovering workaholics experiment with taking more time for relaxation, they may feel guilty for being lazy. And when caretakers start to acknowledge and express their own needs, instead of taking care of others, they may feel selfish. As we deviate from the norms and patterns of our socialized persona, it is natural that we will experience guilt feelings. Developing a tolerance for these feelings will enable us to continue the process of integrating the shadow.

Guilt is part and parcel of being human and of making choices. In fact, normal guilt is a healthy sign that we are responsible and caring human beings. Unlike neurotic guilt, which is really not guilt but rather fear of what others will think, or the total inability to feel guilt, which is a character disorder, normal guilt reflects the fact that we are social beings for whom relations with others are important. It challenges us to examine our choices and actions and keeps us honest about our motives. If we try to live in such a way as to avoid guilt feelings, we will stop growing. The need to "be good," to be pure, to have no faults is appropriate to childhood, when the young ego is frail and consciousness is just beginning to develop. Too much guilt in early life can leave us fearful and overly cautious, always needing to be seen by others as a "good girl" or "good boy." Integrating the shadow requires a strong ego because it brings us up against the parental "shoulds" and "should nots" that we have internalized as the voice of conscience, even the voice of God.

This process of psychological separation or differentiation can "feel wrong" when we first begin it. We can feel as if we are doing a "bad thing" when we begin to do "our own thing." Fairy tales and myths sometimes make this point by showing how the protagonist must "steal" something as part of the process of coming to wholeness. Robert Bly's *Iron John*, for instance, illustrates how the young man has to "steal" the key from under his mother's pillow, symbolizing a psychological independence from his mother. Numerous fairy tales have a similar theme and show what can happen when people meet or fail to meet the challenges their development requires.

RECLAIMING THE HIDDEN TREASURE

There is a wealth of energy bound up in the shadow. When it is made conscious, that energy is available to use as we choose. A client discovered the truth of this when he had a dream that dramatically exposed his shadow and felt charged with new energy as a result of that discovery.[12] The man was a successful professional in his mid-forties. A devoted family man, a good provider, and a regular churchgoer, he was troubled that he was not socially responsible enough. For years he toyed with the idea of leaving his secure job and striking out on his own in a more risky but potentially more fulfilling work. However, when push came to shove, he was never able to make the move; his nerves always failed him. He also experienced an inability at home either to conform to his wife's many demands and expectations or to openly disagree with her. During a therapy session, he recounted the following dream:

> I am struggling across some rough terrain, hilly. I cross a deep ravine and then have to cross a rushing river. I somehow get across, cold and exhausted, and see a house. I enter the house, go through it into another house. An older friendly man is there. He gives me some dry clothes to put on and some hot tea. There is a sharp pointed file lying on the table. I pick it up and kill him with it.

The dream clearly reflects the emergence of shadow aspects and suggests a heretofore unlived, unavailable aspect of this individual's self. The client reported that he awoke from the dream in a highly excited and emotional state—with tears, but not of sadness or distress about his dream. Sensing that the dream was important, he was eager to discuss it with his analyst. He was unclear whom the victim in the dream represented, though he thought it could be his father or his analyst. Nevertheless, thoughts of the dream filled him with strong emotions for days. The subsequent change in the client's behavior suggests how his nocturnal encounter with his shadow fueled his life with new energy:

> In the days that followed the dream he felt himself to be freed somehow. He had an angry, mildly physical confrontation with his wife when she attempted to interfere with an activity he had arranged with his son. He reported that he was able for the first time to tell her how much he resented her intrusion and her managerial bullying and he was able for the first time to tell me [his therapist] how much he disliked therapy—the resentment and humiliation he felt about having to reveal things about himself to me that no one else knew.... He became increasingly involved and fascinated with rather risky "wheeler-dealer" business transactions involving large sums of money. He showed a considerable flair for these activities and considerable success.

When we face our shadow squarely, we not only discover hidden potentials for new ways of feeling and acting, but also that our strong negative feelings are not as threatening to our well-being as once feared.

INTEGRATION LEADS TO WHOLENESS

Integrating the shadow is a way of becoming more fully the person God created us to be. When we engage ourselves in the work of becoming more conscious, we do so with the goal not of ridding ourselves of the shadow but of including it, giving it a place in our identity. We never fully integrate the shadow, but rather grow in our capacity to recognize it. In fact, if we had no shadow, we would be the poorer for its absence, because without it we would be flat and dull, lacking in substance and personality. We are enriched by the shadow; it makes us interesting, gives us depth and character, and strengthens our sense of identity. The more we know ourselves, the less fearful and defensive we need be. True self-knowledge is grounding. It gives us a sense of security and self-confidence that frees us to be ourselves, even at the risk of others' disapproval. Integrating the shadow has the effect of enhancing our being, of making us more fully human and alive. Our bodies also benefit from shadow work. Chronic body tension and other physical ailments seem to diminish as repressed energies are allowed to surface and are given constructive outlets. As creative energies once bound up in the shadow become available to us, we may find, to our surprise, that we have more potential and enthusiasm for life than we had imagined.

The redemption of the shadow also has a profound effect on our spiritual life. For as we look at what frightens and shames us and come to know the pain that made us reject ourselves in the first place, we become newly receptive to God's healing grace. Being able to bring all of ourselves to God in prayer releases us from the need to prove ourselves to God. As God's love for those wounded parts of us sinks in, we are able, perhaps for the first time, to love ourselves, dark side and all. We also find ourselves more able to reach out in love and compassion to others because we are less self-righteous and judgmental. When this happens, we have taken a monumental step toward reclaiming the wholeness of that 360-degree personality that was once ours. As we replace our one-sided emphasis on goodness with a more healthy and productive ethic of wholeness, we will also be contributing to bringing about peace in our world. For, in the words of a Jungian writer, "The individual who can manage not to be psychologically infectious—that is, free of the unconscious necessity to project all of his inferior, dark qualities onto others or onto ideologies or causes—is the individual on whom the ultimate peace of the world rests."[13]

Reflection Questions

1. Using Robert Bly's image of the shadow as a bag filled with rejected aspects of the self, whereby our 360-degree personality is reduced to a small portion of what it could be, describe how this "bag stuffing" has taken place through the course of your life.

2. A fruitful way of praying with scripture is to identify with different gospel figures. Using the parable of the prodigal son (Lk 15:11-32), describe the personality traits and qualities of the younger son and the older son. With which one of these sons would you identify? Which one seems just the opposite of who you are?

Reflect on your answers in light of this: the son with whom you identify represents your ego personality; the other son represents your shadow. Given this, what can you learn about your shadow?

In a similar way, contemplate with your imagination the passage about Mary and Martha (Lk 10:38-42). Get a feel for how differently the two sisters act in this situation. How would you describe the personality of each sister? Do you identify with Mary or with Martha? Which sister seems most unlike you? What can you learn about shadow aspects of yourself through this reflection?

3. Share your experience of how the shadow causes problems in relationships and group life. Give specific examples.

CHAPTER THREE

CODEPENDENCY:

A BETRAYAL OF WHOLENESS

Codependents are "persons without centers."[1]
–Virginia Curran Hoffman
THE CODEPENDENT CHURCH

CODEPENDENCY INVOLVES A PATTERN of thinking, feeling, and behaving that is self-defeating and destructive. As "persons without centers," codependents look to others for a sense of identity and direction. This excessive dependency destroys their ability to live freely as autonomous adults and traps them in painful relationships. The following story illustrates the struggle that codependents experience:

> Once upon a time, a woman moved to a cave in the mountains to study with a guru. She wanted, she said, to learn everything there was to know. The guru supplied her with stacks of books and left her alone so she could study. Every morning, the guru returned to the cave to monitor the woman's progress. In his hand, he carried a heavy wooden cane. Each morning, he asked her the same question: "Have you learned everything there is to know yet?" Each morning, her answer was the same. "No," she said, "I haven't." The guru would then strike her over the head with his cane.
>
> This scenario repeated itself for months. One day the guru entered the cave, asked the same question, heard the same answer, and raised his cane to hit her in the same way, but the woman grabbed the cane from the guru, stopped his assault in midair.
>
> Relieved to end the daily batterings but fearing reprisal, the woman looked up at the guru. To her surprise, the guru smiled.

"Congratulations," he said, "you have graduated. You now know everything you *need* to know."

"How's that?" the woman asked.

"You have learned that you will never learn everything there is to know," he replied. "And you have learned how to stop the pain."[2]

Though codependent behaviors cause us pain, we, like the woman in the cave, repeat them because we are unaware that we have the ability to stop the pain.

The term "codependent" originally referred to persons who were so closely involved with an alcoholic or drug addict that their lives revolved around the addict's behavior. Today the term implies problems with a variety of issues such as self-esteem, setting limits, intimacy skills, and compulsive activity, usually in the form of "helping" others. The literature on codependency suggests personality characteristics that bear a striking resemblance to the caricature of the "good Christian": for example, compulsively putting the needs of others before one's own, an inability to say "no," and an excessive sense of responsibility for the welfare of others.

Addressing the reality of codependency and how it affects our lives and relationships is a necessary aspect of developing a holistic spirituality. We must each discern the extent to which we are codependent and the degree to which we have relinquished control of our lives in order to satisfy others' expectations and needs. Some of us are so dedicated to caring for people that we do not even realize that our own needs are neglected. We may even have been taught that to love like Jesus meant sacrificing ourselves to take care of others. A priest recounts how that lesson was driven home to him in his final year in the seminary: "One of our professors was giving us an inspired fervorino on how we ought to see ourselves in relationship to the Church. 'You should find your greatest joy,' he said, 'in giving yourselves completely to the service of the Church. You should desire no life of your own. You should let yourself be used by the Church in whatever way she needs you.'"[3] According to this spirituality of self-sacrifice, the Christian ideal is to love selflessly, that is, without regard for oneself. Although such lofty altruism attracts the idealist in us, it also distorts the true nature of gospel love which commands us to love God and others as we love ourselves (Mt 22:39). If our spirituality leads us to love others to the point of neglecting ourselves, we will fail to fulfill this twofold commandment and set ourselves up for depression and burnout. We may also become the kind of caregivers who unconsciously serve their own needs in the guise of serving others. In her aptly named book *I Only Want What's Best for You*, Gestalt therapist Judith Brown describes how subtle self-seeking can surface in the course of parenting. When a mother, for example, shows off her new baby, saying "Now I'll never be alone again," or when parents have a child in order to save their marriage, or when a child is used to fill a parent's insatiable craving for affection, then the parenting is not primarily for the child. "No matter how pristine our intentions, how intelligent our approaches, if our parenting is coming through underground channels of our needs," states Brown, "it is inevitable that it will come out contaminated."[4]

An integrated spirituality challenges us to make our way gracefully between the Scylla of narcissism, resulting from excessive self-concern, and the Charybdis of grandiosity, resulting from too easily dismissing our legitimate needs as human beings. When caring for others is not balanced with caring for self, it leads to distorted forms of care, such as doing for people what they can do for themselves, giving assistance to people who do not want or need it, giving help we really do not want to give, or expecting to receive something but not asking for it. These symptoms of codependency can appear in our lives, whether or not we are associated with an addict.

Most of what has been written about dealing with codependency comes from the mental health field and focuses on techniques and programs for recovery. While these resources have grown in popularity and availability, as evidenced in the multiplicity of "self-help" groups, they fall short of providing guidance to Christians who want to know how faith can contribute to healing and recovery. While acknowledging the value of the self-help movement, it is important to recognize its limitations. Theologian Richard Neuhaus, in looking at codependency from the perspective of Christian spirituality, alludes to this when he states that "codependency thinking shares the modern infatuation with technique. Most self-help books...suggest that it is a suitable goal to strive to become a *technician* of the inner life."[5] This chapter suggests otherwise, that is, that the goal of Christian spirituality is not to perfect our inner life but to help us surrender to a God whose love for us heals and frees us from the bondage of codependency. After describing the characteristics of codependency, the second half of this chapter will present ways of using the rich resources of the Christian tradition to facilitate recovery from patterns of codependent thinking and behavior.

CHARACTERISTICS OF CODEPENDENCY

Authorities in the field of codependency agree that the majority of people in our society today are, to some degree, affected by codependency, that is, the tendency to depend on others to supply us with a sense of identity and worth. They suggest that the condition of codependency is so built into the fabric of our institutions that we perceive as normal and acceptable that which is unhealthy and dysfunctional. Critics of codependence theory, on the other hand, argue that the concept is unclearly defined and so all-inclusive as to make it meaningless. One such critic states, "Because there are no valid and reliable measures of codependency, we cannot differentiate the codependent person from anyone else in the population."[6] While the debate over the validity of codependence theory continues in academic circles, there is practical benefit in knowing some of the signs of codependency and how they may manifest themselves in our lives.

COMPULSIVE GIVING

Codependents tend to be self-sacrificing, generous, other-directed, and idealistic people. Since these are also characteristics of genuine self-transcendence, codependency has often been confused with holiness. What distinguishes codependence from authentic Christian behavior is the compulsive quality of the codependent's relationships with others. For the codependent, giving is a "must" rather than a response of genuine compassion. Codependents do not give freely, they give because they "should." The "giving" of the codependent is often more a flight from self than the dying to self that characterizes true Christian service. Suffering from low self-esteem and feelings of being unlovable, codependents strive to overcome these painful feelings by proving to others that they are good and therefore worthy of love. In a culture that equates doing good with being good, codependents easily become addicted to helping others, thereby justifying themselves by good works.

POOR SELF-IMAGE

To the codependent it is of utmost importance that others think well of them, because it is to these same people that the codependent looks for a sense of identity and self-esteem. Lacking a positive connection to their true self, codependents cannot turn inward to this vital source of identity and security and so become dependent on the outer world to give them what they cannot find within. This nagging sense of inner poverty, which differs from the peace that comes from a genuine poverty of spirit, leads codependents to attach themselves to others through making themselves helpful and needed. Being needed by others provides a feeling of value and positive identity for those whose inner world is filled with negative self-images and low self-esteem. It is not difficult to see how codependents become addicted to work or ministry. Their need to be needed makes them acutely sensitive to others' expectations and desires, and their low self-esteem predisposes them to seek their value in doing for others. Their generosity and self-sacrifice is often affirmed and reinforced by their significant others—family, friends, church and colleagues— who come to depend on what the codependent does for them.

COMPENSATORY ACTIVITY

Codependents use activity and relationships to avoid their inner world. The outer-directed focus that characterizes codependency serves as a defense against feeling the emptiness, pain, and anxiety within. The compulsive, self-protective nature of their activity goes unrecognized by codependents because of the gratification and self-worth that they feel in doing things for others. Unlike the contemplative-in-action, whose "doing" flows out of a rich inner life of prayer and discernment, the codependent is moved to action by the urgency of an inner emptiness seeking to be filled. At its core, codependency is a spiritual problem that arises from a lack of healthy self-knowledge and self-love. Unable to believe in their own inherent goodness, codependents find it hard to trust in God's unconditional love for them. When codependents talk about their childhood, they rarely remember any consistent experience of feeling loved and appreciated for being themselves. More often they recall stories in which they were loved only when they met others' expectations and criticized when they failed to do so, leaving them with a sense of shame and failure.

SHAME

Shame plays an important role in the dynamics of the codependent whose unique personality was never appreciated and validated. Conditional love makes a child feel bad. Eventually such children internalize a sense of shame about themselves and feel that they are to blame for not being good enough to be loved. They learn to hide their true feelings behind a flexible facade that adapts itself to whatever is expected. Thus, the stage is set for a lifelong pattern of self-rejection and abandonment in favor of caring for others. In so doing, the codependent hopes to be found good enough to be cared for in return.

PEOPLE PLEASING

The theme of "not good enough" pervades the codependent's life and feelings. Being human is never good enough for them. They equate incompleteness and imperfection with being unforgivably flawed and believe they must redeem themselves by their own efforts and earn the right to be valued and loved both by God and others. Having never felt loved without condition, codependents lack the innate sense of self-care that would make them sensitive to their own needs. Thus, they are often incapable of finding a balance between activity (doing) and passivity (being). When conditional love and acceptance is all a person has ever known, he or she will continue to search for what has been missed, usually through hard work and pleasing others, and repressing any feelings, impulses, or behaviors that might bring criticism or disapproval. In other words, they cope by being false. This dependency on others' approval imprisons the codependent in a world of pretense and futility, as the following story vividly illustrates:

A father and his son took a donkey to the market. The man sat on the beast and the boy walked. People along the way said, "What a terrible thing: a big strong fellow sitting on the donkey's back while the youngster has to walk." So, the father dismounted and the son took his place. Soon onlookers remarked, "How terrible: the old man walking and the little boy sitting." At that, they both got on the donkey's back—only to hear others say, "How cruel: two people sitting on one little donkey." Off they got. But other bystanders commented, "How crazy: the donkey has nothing on his back and two people are walking." Finally, they both carried the donkey and they never did make it to the market.[7]

PERFECTIONISM

Codependents strive for perfection of self rather than acceptance of self. Haunted by feelings that they are never good enough, they work diligently and endlessly at trying to perfect themselves and their world. Most codependents, because they have never known anything except conditional acceptance and love, believe that they are not acceptable or lovable unless they are perfect. The illusion of perfection permeates their fantasies and plans. They hold idealized goals for themselves and others and are easily discouraged, sometimes enraged, at their own or others' failure to achieve what they imagine. Codependents are particularly prone to depression as a result of their perfectionism. The realization that they cannot control the world plunges them into a state of helplessness and hopelessness which makes them cling all the more to something or someone outside themselves for a sense of security. They sincerely believe that it is possible to achieve perfection if they can just figure out how to do it.

CONTROLLING

The perfectionism of the codependent is also manifested in a style of relationship that is based on control and manipulation rather than honesty and mutuality. When codependents feel insecure and powerless, they compensate by acting the opposite. Codependent people can become adept at managing others in order to get the attention and approval they need. Their painful feelings of helplessness are denied and converted to feelings of power by focusing all their attention on meeting the needs of others. They have a way of getting into others' lives by making themselves needed, and then helping in ways that point to their own generosity and self-sacrifice. Others exist to make the codependent feel needed! Although codependents would be the last to see this shadow side of their helpfulness, they relate to others as objects which they use to give themselves a sense of purpose and value. Another aspect of the dark side of the need of codependents to help others is that they do this in a way that makes others dependent on them. Genuine helping, in contrast to codependent helping, is not primarily self-serving but arises out of genuine empathy and compassion. Because it is a response to another's real need for help, not one's own need to be helpful, it quietly enables those served to become healthier, more autonomous persons. In other words, authentic service, because it is freely given, is liberating and life-giving to all involved.

LIBERATION THROUGH CONTEMPLATION

The condition of codependency is one of being in captivity, of being stuck with self-defeating learned behaviors or character defects that result in addictions, depression, troubled relationships, and chronic dissatisfaction. Christian contemplation can provide a key to freedom and healing. Because the term "contemplation" is variously understood within different spiritual traditions, it would be helpful at the outset to define our use of the term. Here we are not using the term in the Carmelite sense of contemplation as a passive, infused way of praying (à la St. Teresa and St. John of the Cross). Rather, we are following the Ignatian tradition of active contemplation which emphasizes the value of the imagination. The aim of such prayer is to internalize the good news of God's unconditional love and Christ's presence as a source of personal healing. Being contemplative in the Ignatian sense means two things. First, it means taking time off and away for solitude. In this free and friendly space, we can be with ourselves and enjoy a perspective provided by prayer that allows us to be more attentive to the movements of God's grace in our lives. Second, contemplation is the form of prayer by which we actively use our imagination to help us "see" the choices that grace invites us to make in response to the challenges of our life situation.

Prayer also sharpens our sense of the presence of God abiding with us as we take adult responsibility for shaping our lives more and more into the pattern of Jesus' life.

This strategy for freedom relies on the power of reimaging and learning how to transcend inhibiting self-images and to acquire liberating ways of viewing one's life. Escape from bondage begins with the capacity to imagine that things can be other than they are, that things do not have to stay the same. Contemplation nurtures solitude and creativity, which, in turn, give birth to liberating alternatives to debilitating addictions. Suffering in itself will not deliver us from situations in which we feel stuck. Only when we see that there are other possibilities for being and acting and that our present suffering is unnecessary will we mobilize the resources available to us to bring about a change.

Contemplative Solitude

The codependent way of being, because it is primarily reactive to others, lacks the personal freedom and creativity that characterize mature psychological and spiritual development. The codependent (false) self focuses exclusively on the outer world because a life-giving connection to a vital inner world is missing. Holistic spiritual growth requires what the codependent avoids, namely, the solitude and honest self-reflection that create the space and conditions in which intimacy with self, with God, and with others can grow. A common pitfall for codependents is their tendency to mistake their excessively busy schedules and superficial relationships as authentic Christian living and to think themselves exempted from the need for solitude, leisure and prayer. Experiencing themselves as indispensable and sometimes overwhelmed by the demands of their work or ministry, codependents easily fall into the trap of believing that "my work is my prayer." The busy school principal who wearily says, "When I finish this job in a few years, then I'll have time to attend to my spiritual life," is a common example of a sincere person who is unconsciously living in the bondage of codependency. The codependent, if he or she is ever to break out of this inauthentic pattern of living, must begin by recognizing the reciprocal relationship between service and solitude. Just as a genuine spiritual life must issue forth in service, true Christian service must be rooted in prayer and love.

As a corrective to the tendency of codependents to look outside themselves to receive a sense of identity, contemplation invites them to solitude, where the sense of self can be shaped. It is only in the silent matrix of solitude that the unique dimensions of the self are fathomed. Solitude is a time for intimacy with one's self. A graphic description of this aspect of solitude was once provided by a most unlikely source, an eleven year old adolescent. Breaking in on a conversation between his parents about the importance of solitude for the spiritual life, he asked, "Is it like when I go into my room and sit in the corner by myself and the outside noises (like the banging of the pots in the kitchen) get smaller and the inside noises get bigger?" Listening sensitively to one's inner voices, acquainting oneself with the various parts that constitute the self, and befriending the self as good company—all these things are what solitude makes possible. By allowing codependents to get in touch with the currents of their lives, solitude makes an inner life possible. It undergirds a true spirituality because it is an essential condition for at-homeness with oneself and intimacy with God and others.

One of the hallmarks of authentic spiritual and psychological growth is an increase in one's ability to accept and lovingly embrace all of who one is. Johannes Metz speaks of this in his book *Poverty of Spirit* when he says that the hardest task is to accept our human condition. He speaks of a universal temptation to reject our being, to flee from being fully human. He goes so far as to say that this is the reason God had to make it a commandment to love oneself. Perhaps this is a way to understand the nature of sin. It is the rejection of the human condition and the refusal to say "yes" to being incomplete and essentially poor. Codependency, from a spiritual perspective, is a contemporary way of speaking about this denial of creaturehood.

Wholeness and liberation, not perfection and control, are the goals of holistic Christian development. Codependents must learn to shift their focus from the outer world on which they feel so dependent to the inner world in which the unloved child of the past awaits their attention and love. They must learn to invite God, the true source of their identity and security, into their inner poverty and to trust that unconditional Love waits there to embrace them and to transform their shame and pain into the consolation of a

Love that has no requirements or limits. Contemplative prayer is a way by which this transformation can occur.

IMAGINATIVE CONTEMPLATION AND HEALING

Just as codependents can reclaim the self in the regenerative moments provided by solitude, they can also profit by contemplating the scriptures that reveal the healing presence of Christ today. St. Ignatius of Loyola, in his *Spiritual Exercises*, presents a way of praying with scripture that uses the imagination to lead one into a more intimate relationship with the Lord. Called imaginative contemplation, it is similar to the therapeutic method of active imagination used by C. G. Jung to help people become more aware of their unconscious. In imaginative contemplation, we are invited to pray over a gospel scene by moving with our imagination and senses directly into an event and reliving it, as if it were our own experience. This immersion allows the gospel event to spring to life and to involve us actively as participants. When we encounter Jesus this way, we receive an intimate, felt-knowledge of him as a vibrant person, and the gospel events with which we are so familiar take on new meaning for our lives today.

A simple approach to imaginative contemplation with scripture contains three steps. Each moves us into a progressively deeper experience of a mystery of faith. First, the account of an event in scripture, such as the cure of the blind beggar Bartimaeus at the end of the Way section in Mark's gospel (10:46-52), is read. Second, we identify with one of the onlookers and describe the action from his or her point of view. This is done as if the event were actually unfolding right now in front of our eyes. Third, we insert ourselves into the event by identifying with one of the active participants in the scene. As we experience what is happening in the gospel scene, we are advised to be aware of our entire subjective response, of what we are thinking, sensing, and feeling.

As often happens in a psychodrama or a play, there can come a time in contemplation when the artificiality of the put-on identity slips away and the gospel character comes to life in us. Then it is no longer Bartimaeus the blind beggar who is being summoned to Jesus and being healed, but the blind person in us who is being led out of the darkness of personal confusion by the Lord's healing touch. It is no longer Bartimaeus who is crying out with desperation for help, but a desperately blind part of us that seeks enlightenment. Then it is no longer just a study of the historical Jesus interacting with people in biblical times, but the risen Christ healing us today. When our contemplation shifts from imaginative role playing to spontaneous identification, we are drawn into a graced encounter with the risen Christ today.

Imaginative contemplation can bring hope to the struggling codependent. Theologian William Spohn captures the value of contemplating scripture through the method of identification with gospel characters when he states,

> As we tangibly and visually move into their narrated encounter with the Lord, we find in ourselves some echo of their response: If Peter could be forgiven, so can I. If the father could welcome home the prodigal son, then my fears of God's anger are without foundation. We learn to "ask for what we want" in these contemplations by the example of these characters in the story. They raise our expectations and open us to hear the Lord's word to us today.[8]

For codependents, an important value of imaginative contemplation is that it trains them to spot the similarities existing between scriptural events and their own life experiences. By helping them identify the analogy between biblical situations and their own, it moves them from the memory of God's intervention in the past to a perception of divine intervention in their present crisis. Catching this rhyme between past and present becomes a liberating insight for those who are blinded by codependency.

INTERNALIZING THE LOVE OF GOD

Imaginative contemplation can be a powerful way for codependents to hear the word of God being addressed to them in the present. This method of prayer connects them with aspects of themselves that have been unconsciously repressed or consciously suppressed in order to cope with childhood wounds or present pain. In either case, disowning parts of themselves is like saying to members of the family that there is no place for them at home. It is a denial of the total self that leads to self-alienation and fragmentation. When codependent tendencies make us suppress parts of ourselves, we not only blot them out of our minds, but also exclude them from our prayer. Thus, we keep these wounded parts out of God's healing reach. The struggle for wholeness is greatly supported by prayer, once we acknowledge our fragmented state and let our struggling parts be addressed by the word of God.

When we begin to pray in this way, we are usually surprised by the sudden emergence of suppressed parts demanding attention. The attention these disowned aspects need is not only ours, but also God's. Contemplative prayer allows the word of God to address these rejected parts with the good news of the Savior's affirming love. In the safety of prayer, for example, our codependent self, like Nicodemus under the safe cover of darkness, can surface to meet the Lord. The dejected part wallowing in self-hatred can hear God say as God said to Jesus at the River Jordan, "You are my...beloved; my favor rests on you" (Mk 1:11). The compulsive helper in us, which anxiously and manically rushes about taking care of things, can be calmed by hearing Yahweh's quiet reassurance: "Be still and know that I am God" (Ps 46:10). The wounded inner child can drop the pretense of being perfect and hear Yahweh say, "I regard you as precious, since you are honored and I love you" (Is 43:4). The chronic worrier of sleepless nights can find consolation in the good shepherd's assurance that "there is no need to be afraid, little flock, for it has pleased your Father to give you the kingdom" (Lk 12:32). The shameful part can let its confusion and guilt be dissolved by the unconditional acceptance of Jesus, who says to it what he said to the adulterous woman, "Has no one condemned you?...Neither do I condemn you" (Jn 8:10-11). By allowing these parts to approach the Lord in the intimacy of prayer, imaginative contemplation can help codependents experience a powerfully transforming encounter with the living word of God.

St. Ignatius hoped that using the method of imaginative contemplation would bring us "felt-knowledge" (*sentir*) of God's love for us, not merely "head-knowledge." This personal knowledge goes beyond grasping something conceptually or intellectually, but involves realizing something emotionally, in a way that affects our whole being. Felt-knowledge is something we know from direct, immediate experience, not from reading or hearsay. In other words, what we desire in contemplating scripture is an experience by which we know "in our bones" that God loves us with unconditional and unwavering love. The following prayer exercises are designed to help us to know in our hearts that we are the beloved of God.

A. *Being the Beloved*

Biblical Passage

The Baptism of Jesus in the Jordan (Mk 1:9-11; Mt 3:13-17; Lk 3: 21-22)

Prayer Experience

1. Find a quiet place, where you can be alone and undisturbed for a period of thirty to forty-five minutes.

2. Say a brief prayer acknowledging the presence of God as you enter into prayer and ask for the grace to be open to being touched by God.

3. Read the text a couple of times slowly, and take in the event that the text is relating: What is happening and how does the action unfold? Who are the people involved? How do they feel about each other and what is occurring?

4. Put the text away. Now with your imagination, see the dramatic action of the scene unfold, as if you were witnessing the event as an outside observer.

5. Notice especially what Jesus experiences as his cousin, John the Baptist, pours water on his forehead. Imagine Jesus' looking up and seeing the heavens part and then hearing the voice of the Creator of the universe say to him: "You are my beloved in whom I take great delight." As Jesus takes in what is happening to him, imagine his whole body being filled with the warm glow and fullness of God's affirming love.

6. Next, put yourself at the edge of the riverbank and imagine yourself somehow being drawn to John the Baptist to be baptized and to enjoy the same experience that Jesus had. Imagine yourself tentatively dipping your feet into the river and feeling the soft mud at the river's bottom ooze gently through your toes. Then you start to move toward the middle more boldly because you find the water warm and welcoming. Then see yourself standing in line, waiting your turn. Suddenly you find yourself in front of the Baptist and he starts to pour water on your forehead. At that moment, you look up and see the heavens part and you hear the voice of the Creator of the

universe say to *you*: "You are my beloved in whom I take great delight." When you hear these words, you feel your whole body warm up with the glow of God's affirming love. Remain in that moment and absorb what has just been addressed to you. Allow God's reassuring voice to resonance deeply throughout your being, filling up your inner pockets of emptiness and pain with healing love.

Comments on the Exercise

Because our compulsive behavior as codependents is often fueled by feelings of inner emptiness, inadequacy, and shame, we need the healing grace of seeing ourselves as we are in God's eyes: lovable and acceptable. The very sight of us delights God. It is noteworthy that Jesus received his affirming experience of divine favor at the River Jordan *before* the start of his public ministry. This fact highlights the truth that God's love for us, as it was for Jesus, is based on our being, not on our doing. Like Jesus, we are the apple of God's eyes. God's love created us and continues to sustain us every moment of our existence. We are the beloved of God, simply because God has chosen us to enjoy that status, not because we in any way have earned it by our personal qualities or achievements.

B. An Experience of Being Mirrored

Biblical Passage

The Presentation of Jesus in the Temple (Lk 2:22-38)

Prayer Experience

1. Begin by following steps 1-4 of prayer exercise "A" above, "Being the Beloved."

2. With the eyes of your imagination, see Joseph and Mary with the infant Jesus in her arms climbing the steep steps of the temple in Jerusalem. As they enter the section of the temple where the child is to be presented to God, a holy man named Simeon approaches them. Moving aside the cloth covering the baby's face, he bends close to get a good look at the child. Notice how he beams with joy and excitement as he looks long and lovingly into the infant's eyes. He then straightens up and, with a heart bursting with gratitude and praise, he prays:

Now, Master, you are letting your servant go in peace
as you promised;
for my eyes have seen the salvation
which you have made ready in the sight of the nations;
a light of revelation for the Gentiles
and glory for your people Israel.

3. Just as Simeon finishes praying, Anna, the eighty-four year old prophetess who spent her days in the temple serving God with fasting and prayer, comes by. She too looks long and lovingly at the child Jesus and breaks out in praise because she sees in the face of this baby the promised messiah, sent by God to establish the kingdom of God.

4. Notice how the infant Jesus is so alert and attentive to both Simeon and Anna as they hover over him with admiration and love. Their warm smiles, gentle touch, and adoring eyes fill Jesus with a deep sense of being special and loved.

5. Now imagine that you are the infant in Mary's arms. Joseph is there, as are Simeon and Anna. They draw gently near to you and, by turn, ask to hold you. As you are passed from one person to the next, you see your own lovableness and specialness reflected in the eyes of these adults who bend over you with such obvious affection and appreciation. Imagine how their affirming reactions fill your being with a deep sense of your goodness.

Comments on the Exercise

Many of us are driven to codependent behaviors by an underlying, often unconscious, feeling that we are not good enough to be loved and accepted for who we are. In order to gain love and win approval, we become addicted to helping others and making ourselves indispensable. This deficit in self-esteem often stems from childhood experiences of emotional deprivation. The theme of the inner child or the "child within" has been developed by such theorists as W. Hugh Missildine, M.D. and Eric Berne, M.D. to describe a conscious, consistent pattern of thoughts, feelings, attitudes, and behaviors that resemble or re-create the experience a person had as an actual child. The term is popularly used in such self-help groups as Adult Children of Alcoholics (ACA) to help people better understand their sense of emotional deprivation and emptiness, stemming from childhood experiences of neglect, abuse, or abandonment in dysfunctional families.[9]

As children, we need to receive confirming responses from the significant others in our lives regarding our specialness and lovableness. This explains why children often want to be the center of attention, actively seek the praise of others for their accomplishments, and yearn to be the apple of their parents' eyes. When our parents or primary caregivers do not mirror our specialness in a way that satisfies this need, our ability to feel lovable and attractive is gravely impaired. Psychologists refer to this impairment as a "narcissistic wound." Imaginative prayer, such as the above two exercises, can contribute to the healing of the deep hurt that results from not having received adequate mirroring in childhood.

C. Our Past Hurts and the Love of God

Biblical Passage
Jesus and the Children (Mk 10:13-16)

Prayer Experience
1. Begin by following steps 1-4 of prayer exercise "A" above, "Being the Beloved."

2. With the eyes of your imagination, see how parents are rushing up to Jesus, bringing their little children for him to touch. Seeing this, the disciples react quickly to stop them because they are concerned that Jesus needs some time alone to rest. But Jesus scolds the disciples for trying to prevent the children from coming close to him. Notice how Jesus reaches out and hugs each of the children. Then he lays his hands on them and blesses them. Experience how secure and loved each child feels as he or she is being embraced and blessed by Jesus.

3. Now imagine that you are taking your childhood hurts to Jesus so that they too can be touched. Just as you arrive, Jesus is blessing the last of the children gathered around him and the disciples. You walk up and stand right in front of him. Jesus smiles warmly at you and invites you to sit next to him. You hesitate and slowly move closer. Putting his arm around your shoulders, he encourages you to tell him how you have been hurt. As the compassionate and understanding

face of Jesus acknowledges the hurts you have experienced, you feel deeply reassured of your own lovableness.

Comments on the Exercise

Often the narcissistic wound felt by codependents stems from not having been touched and seen as children in a way that reassured them of their goodness and lovableness. Warm and caring touch is important for the healthy development of infants. As a hospital bulletin puts it in reporting how its "volunteer cuddler program" is flourishing, "Recent studies in the neonatal intensive care units of several hospitals indicate that infants who are regularly held, stroked and spoken to gain weight faster and leave the hospital sooner than those who are not."[10] If there is a place in us that feels that it was not "regularly held, stroked and spoken to," praying over the passage of Jesus and the children, using imaginative contemplation, can be a way of opening this hurt part of us to God's healing grace.

D. Fear of Abandonment and the Love of God

Some of us codependents are also burdened with the fear of rejection and abandonment. In intimate relationships, we find ourselves always fearful of being dropped and left behind. This fear sometimes originates in childhood when we experienced ourselves abandoned, either physically or emotionally. Children sometimes feel abandoned when they are physically separated from a parent because of death, divorce, or displacement due to war or economic necessity. Children can also feel isolated and bereft when their parents' problems with addiction, unemployment or illness consume so much time and energy that they have little left to give to their needy children. For those of us who have experienced such abandonment in childhood, the above prayer exercise of Jesus and the children would be profitably continued with the following steps:

1. Imagine yourself as a small child sitting on Jesus' lap. Sense how Jesus intuits your discomfort with intimacy and fear of being rejected and abandoned.

2. Wanting to comfort and reassure you, Jesus tells you of God's love for you. Like a parent soothing a fearful child by reading it a story, Jesus recites the following verses from the prophet Isaiah:

For Zion was saying, "Yahweh has abandoned me,
the Lord has forgotten me."
Does a woman forget her baby at the breast,
or fail to cherish the child of her womb?
Yet even if these forget,
I will never forget you.

See I have branded you on the palms of my hands,
your ramparts are always under my eye. (49:14-16)

3. Imagine that your anxiety and fear of abandonment dissipate as you listen to Jesus' gentle reminder of God's faithful love for you.

E. Called by Name

Biblical Passage

The Appearance to Mary of Magdala (Jn 20:11-18)

Prayer Experience

1. Begin by following steps 1-4 of "Being the Beloved" prayer exercise.

2. With the eyes of your imagination, see Mary outside of the tomb of Jesus, weeping. She peers inside the open tomb and finds Jesus' body missing. Two angels in white sitting where the body of Jesus had been ask her, "Woman, why are you weeping?" "They have taken my Lord away," she replies, "and I don't know where they have put him." Turning suddenly, she sees Jesus standing there, though she does not recognize him. Jesus says, "Woman, why are you weeping? Whom are you looking for?" Mistaking him for the gardener, Mary answers, "Sir, if you have taken him away, tell me where you have put him, and I will go and remove him." Jesus says "Mary!" At that moment, hearing Jesus say her name, she recognizes Jesus and reaches out to him.

3. Now imagine that you are roaming about the garden of your ordinary life, feeling depressed, lonely, and empty. Suddenly you bump into a stranger who, to your surprise, calls you by your name. The very moment you hear the loving and endearing way your name is called out, you recognize the risen Jesus and are filled with consolation.

Comments on the Exercise

Mary of Magdala, like others whose encounter with the risen Jesus is described in the resurrection narratives, is meant to be a figure or type with whom all of us are called to identify. Her experience, in other words, is meant also to be ours. Her recognition of the risen Lord is triggered by her hearing a familiar and endearing voice call her name. This account in chapter 20 of John's gospel is charged with added meaning when we hear it in light of what Jesus said ten chapters before when describing himself as the good shepherd:

> I am the good shepherd;
> I know my own and my own know me (10:14)....

> The sheep that belong to me listen to my voice;
> I know them and they follow me (10:27).

In this prayer exercise, we ask for the grace to recognize the voice of the risen Jesus calling out our name with warm affirmation and acceptance, just as he spoke Mary's name in the garden. An experience such as this can bring healing to the wound caused by not feeling seen, recognized, and valued for who we uniquely are.

FROM CODEPENDENCY TO CONTEMPLATION

Contemplation releases the stranglehold of perfectionism by exposing flawlessness as a false condition for self-acceptance and God's love. By focusing our attention on God's personal and infinite love for us, contemplation helps us to accept that the Spirit's creative power is continually working in us, not demanding that we be perfect, but desiring that we become whole. Contemplation opens the ears of our codependent self to the good news of Christian spirituality: that we are creatures who are by nature radically unfinished and yet filled with stunning grace, that our personhood is oriented to completions that are received rather than achieved.

Contemplation is a way of activating the imagination for the sake of personal freedom. It is a time when we are challenged to see how the Lord of history, who unshackled the Israelites from Egyptian chains, continues to be available to us in our experience of captivity. Contemplation is letting the great saving event of the exodus become a pattern of understanding life. During contemplation, people are invited to see the analogy between events of biblical times and their own lives, to spot the similarity between the God who liberated the Israelites from Pharaoh's power and the one who now stands in their lives with the same desire and power to liberate.

Contemplation ultimately invites codependents to foster a healthy reliance on God, the radically Other who is for us. Paradoxically, dependency on God is unlike all forms of immature dependency that leave the person "taken care of" feeling inadequate and impotent. On the contrary, dependency on God allows enabling grace and the reassurance of divine assistance to motivate codependents to take charge of their lives as competent adults. As they become more and more convinced through contemplation of their intrinsic value in God's eyes, they will be better able to claim the right and freedom to live abundant lives.

Reflection Questions

1. Review the section on "Characteristics of Codependency" and share your experience of how these characteristics may show up in your own life and in the lives of those with whom you live and work.

2. Identify an area in your life in which you feel stuck and hopeless. Now imagine concretely how things can be different, can be other than they presently are. Does the vision of a new possibility make you less accepting of the present condition and more motivated to effect a change?

3. Experiment with the prayer experiences suggested in this chapter. Write down in a journal what happened in your prayer and how you were moved. Share these prayer experiences with someone who might benefit from them.

CHAPTER FOUR

PERFECTIONISM:
A PSEUDO-WHOLENESS

What an inestimable grace it is to recognize and appreciate all that is good
enough in ourselves and in our lives! Good enough for our love, loyalty,
dedication, and humble gratitude. Good enough insists there is something
between perfection and mediocrity.[1]
—Leo Rock, S.J.
MAKING FRIENDS WITH YOURSELF

THE ZEN MASTER sent the disciple away from the meditation hall to
pray the mantra, "What I am is enough. What I have is enough."
This Zen teaching was meant to replace the disciple's perfectionistic
strivings with a peaceful acceptance of himself. Many of us can
benefit from this teaching, because we too find ourselves plagued
by a perfectionism that makes us rigid and fearful of being
ourselves. When we pursue perfection, we treat ourselves as if we
were things whose worth would be maximized by being flawless.
Spiritually and psychologically, we pay a high price for our perfectionism. Spiritually, it robs us of peace of soul by torturing us
with unremitting self-criticism. It also deafens us to the good news
that we are unconditionally accepted by a loving and forgiving God.
Psychologically, perfectionism is associated with a wide variety of
problems, including alcoholism, eating and digestive disorders,
depression, writer's block, obsessive-compulsive personality, and
Type A coronary-prone behavior.[2] We do not have to look very far to
find the harmful results of perfectionism.

PERFECTIONISM VERSUS STRIVING FOR EXCELLENCE

When we speak of perfectionism, we are not referring to the pursuit of excellence that motivates many talented people. Appreciating our potential and taking genuine pleasure in striving to meet high standards is healthy. Demanding a higher level of performance than we can obtain smacks of perfectionism. When we have expectations that are unreasonable and unreachable, we strain compulsively and relentlessly toward impossible goals. Perfectionism makes us measure our worth by our productivity and accomplishments. It is that voice in us that says we have not done enough and therefore do not deserve to feel satisfied. In contrast, when we take pleasure in doing our best without needing to be perfect, we can be satisfied with our efforts, even when there is room for improvement. When we are in the grip of perfectionism, we often feel anxious, confused, and emotionally drained before a new task is even begun. We are motivated not so much by desire for improvement as by fear of failure. On the other hand, when we strive for excellence in a healthy way, we are more likely to feel excited, energized, and clear about what needs to be done. In general, the normal quest for excellence is growthful for us as individuals and benefits society as a whole, whereas the compulsive drive for perfection is debilitating and pathological. We need to care passionately about doing things well, but we also need to know how to be gentle with ourselves when we fall short.

Perfectionism is characterized by certain dysfunctional ways of thinking known as "cognitive styles."[3] When we are in a perfectionistic mode, we tend to think dichotomously, which means that we see things in a polarized fashion (e.g. in "either-or," "black-or-white," "always-or-never" terms). Such a cognitive style leads easily to the tendency to overgeneralize (e.g. concluding from one job failure that we are fated to be a failure forever). Furthermore, we fall victim to what Karen Horney termed the "tyranny of shoulds," an overly active system of self-commands. Our perfectionistic consciousness is swamped by "I should" statements. Common examples of such inner dictates are: "I should be the perfect parent, teacher, spouse"; "I should never get angry"; "I should always do the right thing, know the right answer." Finally, we have little compassion for ourselves and are harshly self-critical and overly self-evaluative.

RELIGIOUS CONDITIONING

While the perfectionistic attitude is so remarkably widespread that it can be seen as a cultural phenomenon, it is strongly reinforced for Christians by certain religious factors. First, the biblical injunction to "be perfect as your heavenly Father is perfect" (Mt 5:48) has through the ages given Christians the impression that holiness consists in being a flawless paragon of virtue.

Second, expectations for perfection are often intentionally or unintentionally, consciously or unconsciously communicated to Christian churchgoers. A study by two psychologists points out that "often an unrealistic and unbiblical message of how to live the 'Christian life' is sent in the church."[4]

> If pastors intend for their behavior to be modeled, it is understandable that only their best behaviors and accomplishments are openly displayed. The outcome is that pastoral perfection is modeled to imperfect parishioners.... The potent message sent is "you need to be a perfect Christian." The attending assumption is the need to be completely successful or competent especially in overcoming all personal struggles and limitations.[5]

This message creates a mentality that equates spirituality with perfection. If being imperfect is tantamount to being unspiritual, then avoiding imperfection becomes a goal of Christian life. To be a good Christian then requires that our personal struggles and temptations be hidden from others and often even from ourselves.

Just as some pastors have a proclivity for expecting perfection of their parishioners, parishioners also often send messages that the pastor should be perfect. By putting priests and ministers on a pedestal, the congregation imposes perfectionistic standards on those who serve them in leadership. Vulnerability to perfectionism is compounded when ministers have internalized saintly expectations for themselves. Ordained ministers whose principal role-image consists in being an *alter Christus* ("another Christ") and who have this self-image reinforced by people who revere them as hierarchically just below God are apt examples of the complex dynamics operating in perfectionism.

A third factor that makes Christians particularly vulnerable to perfectionism is the rhetoric of religious life. For example, in Jesuit documents, there is an exhortation to strive always for the *magis* ("the more") and to do everything *ad majorem Dei gloriam* ("for the *greater* glory of God"). Sisters of St. Joseph are given a hundred "maxims of perfection" to follow. Also held up for emulation have been young and idealistic saints, such as St. Stanislaus Kostka, whose motto was *ad majora natus sum* ("I was born for *greater* things"). Without necessarily intending to, users of this kind of exhortatory language can instill in people a sense that what they have accomplished is never enough, that more needs always to be done. The underlying message of much traditional hagiography is that saints are perfect, and, hence, we should all strive for perfection. Commenting on St. John Berchmans after the saint's death, his rector wrote: "What we universally admired in him was that in all the virtues he showed himself perfect and that, with the aid of divine grace to which he responded to his utmost, he performed all his actions with all the perfection that can be imagined."[6]

SYMPTOMS OF PERFECTIONISM

Because perfectionism is culturally sanctioned and built into the fabric of our institutions, we may fail to notice when we have crossed the line between a healthy striving for excellence and perfectionistic demands for achievements. There are, however, any number of symptoms that are indicative of perfectionism. The most common are depression and low self-esteem, procrastination, obsessive-compulsive behavior, fear of failure, troubled relationships, poor self-control, and addictive behaviors.

Depression and Lowered Self-Esteem: Clinical evidence suggests that perfectionistic attitudes lead to depression. One study found that perfectionists "are likely to respond to the perception of failure or inadequacy with a precipitous loss in self-esteem that can trigger episodes of severe depression and anxiety."[7]

Procrastination: It is typical of perfectionists to procrastinate. Because of their self-doubt and unrealistic expectations, they feel defeated and helpless before beginning even ordinary tasks. These feelings make them procrastinate, thereby avoiding the failure that they dread.

Obsessive-Compulsive Behavior: Perfectionists ruminate about past mistakes and worry excessively about future ones. Because they go over and over the same thoughts in their mind, either rehashing the past or rehearsing the future, their thinking style is called obsessive. The anxiety and fear that are behind their obsessive thoughts move them into action in an attempt to relieve the anxiety. This accounts for the strain and drivenness that we experience in perfectionists.

Fear of Failure: Another symptom of perfectionism is the need to play it safe. Since mistakes mean that one is a failure and failure leads to rejection by others, perfectionists find it difficult to try anything new unless they are guaranteed a successful outcome.

Troubled Relationships: Expectations that others live up to their standards cause tension and strain between perfectionists and others. When problems do arise, perfectionists prefer to withdraw rather than risk the rejection they fear from others. For this reason, perfectionism often leads to loneliness and isolation.

Poor Self-Control: Perfectionists often adopt self-management programs, e.g. dieting or exercising, that are so rigorous that they set themselves up for failure. Their initial rigid self-control deteriorates when they experience their first lapse in their overambitious program. This lapse "is viewed as indicating total failure which usually results in binge smoking, drinking, or eating (the 'saint or sinner' syndrome)."[8] Here we see an example of the dichotomous and over-generalized thinking that can lead to the poor self-control. One of the ironies of perfectionism is that when perfectionists fail in perfect self-control, they lose all self-control. A bit of wisdom to help counter this all-or-nothing tendency comes in this Weight Watchers' motto: "Progress, not perfection."

Addictive Behaviors: Addictions of all kinds often mask the need to be perfect. Food, alcohol, drugs, sex, shopping, and relationships are common palliatives for the pain that perfectionists experience when they fail to live up to their unrealistic and idealized self-image.

The symptoms of perfectionism, in one way or another, all express a rejection of human nature and life as limited and incomplete. At the core of perfectionism is a spiritual longing for transcendence that must find its fulfillment in God, not in some self-created perfection.

PERFECTION AS A SPIRITUAL LONGING

Jung believed that the human soul has an inborn need for God that is as powerful and urgent as the instinct for food and drink. This religious urge which directs us toward God must be satisfied if we are to be psychologically healthy. When this fundamental function of the psyche is blocked, we create false gods and give ourselves over to them to the detriment of our spiritual life. Jungian analyst Marion Woodman suggests that striving for perfection is an attempt to meet this religious need, albeit through a counterfeit spirituality. The addict, for example, is trying to unite with God, but seeks this union through a material or created substance. This is the condition of many people today who no longer have a living connection to a faith life that can mediate their spiritual longings. The image of "the perfect," which was once projected onto God, is now projected onto a human being or onto a substance (i.e. food, alcohol, sex). Objects of addiction provide transitory experiences of wholeness, or satisfaction of longings, thus creating illusions of spiritual completeness. Woodman suggests that perfectionism stems from a cultural overemphasis on the masculine principle and a suppression of the feminine. "Essentially I am suggesting," states Woodman, "that many of us—men and women—are addicted in one way or another because our patriarchal culture emphasizes specialization and perfection. Driven to do our best at school, on the job, in our relationships—in every corner of our lives—we try to make ourselves into works of art. Working so hard to create our own perfection we forget that we are human beings."[9] In short, she relates perfectionism to the domination of masculine consciousness. Symbolized by the head, the masculine principle values order, power, and perfection, while the feminine, symbolized by the heart, cherishes feelings, relationships, and mystery. The core issue regarding the problem of perfectionism is, in Woodman's words: "How do goal-oriented perfectionists find their way back to the lost relationship to their own heart?"

ROOTS OF PERFECTIONISM

Finding our way back to our own hearts means going back to childhood to understand how we first began to lose touch with our inner life of feelings. According to a variety of theories, the seeds of perfectionism are planted early on in the human psyche.[10] Cognitive theories suggest that children may develop perfectionistic tendencies by interacting with adults who are perfectionistic. Jung believed that the image of perfection is present at birth, that there is an archetype of perfection, like a Platonic form, in the human (collective) unconscious which acts as an instinct driving us toward perfection. Alfred Adler originally postulated a "will to superiority," which was thought to develop in order to compensate for a sense of inferiority. He later revised this notion and explained it as a "striving for perfection," which could be pathological or healthy depending on the motive underlying it. If the motive was personal security, it was a neurotic or pathological striving. If the motive was religious, that is, serving others out of a sense of social interest and responsibility, it was healthy. Erik Erikson believed that the onset of perfectionism can occur in the elementary school years when children are in the "industry versus inferiority" stage of development. Children who do not experience success in the school and home tasks expected of them develop a hypersensitivity to imperfection because, on the basis of their flawed performance, they conclude that they are inferior. Feeling that they have disappointed the expectations of parents and teachers, they are driven to win the approval of adults by performing perfectly.

Psychoanalytic theorists generally view perfectionism as the result of a harsh superego. They suggest that children growing up in homes where parents are critical and unpredictable feel great anxiety and hostility. Perfectionism becomes a way of coping with such feelings because it allows the child to convert threatening emotions and impulses into behaviors that will be more acceptable to the parents and thus win the love and approval that the child longs for.

THE TYRANNY OF THE SHOULD

Karen Horney's notion of "the tyranny of the should" is perhaps the most useful of all these theories in explaining the dynamics of perfectionism. According to her, perfectionism originates as a coping device adopted by children who "fight against the action of neurotic parents." These parents are unable to provide the affirmation and approval that the children need for the development of a positive sense of self.[11] Unaffirmed children not only feel deep self-doubt but also intense anxiety and anger, which they suppress because they fear retaliation. These "bad" feelings then get directed inward against the self. And then because children equate feeling bad with being bad, they start to feel that they are "not good enough." Helpless and intimidated by parents whom they perceive as all-powerful and hostile, they learn to accommodate. Specifically, the accommodation entails acquiring a better or idealized self to replace the "not-good-enough self." To make up for deep feelings of inadequacy, they unconsciously create a glorified self-image, endowed with inflated and unlimited powers. Eventually they come to identify with this grandiose image. Horney describes how this leads to the emergence of "the tyranny of the should" in the neurotic personality:

> The neurotic sets to work to mold himself into a supreme being of his own making. He holds before his soul his image of perfection and unconsciously tells himself: "Forget about the disgraceful creature you actually are; this is how you should be; and to be this idealized self is all that matters. You should be able to endure everything, to understand everything, to like everybody, to be always productive"—to mention only a few of these inner dictates. Since they are inexorable, I call them "the tyranny of the should."[12]

NEUROTIC VERSUS NARCISSISTIC PERFECTIONISM

So far we have been discussing what psychologists refer to as neurotic perfectionism. There is, however, another form of perfectionism that differs not only in origin, but also in meaning. It has been called "narcissistic perfectionism." A spiritual director or therapist who is trying to help a person overcome perfectionistic tendencies must be able to distinguish between the two types, because the treatment approach for each is quite different. Theoretically, neurotic perfectionists are individuals who have a stable and cohesive sense of self that is relatively independent of outside influences. In other words, they possess a sense of identity that is separate and distinct from parents and others and experience themselves as autonomous moral agents. Their perfectionism is a consequence of trying to live up to the demands of a harsh superego, which punishes them with guilt and loss of self-esteem when they fail to comply perfectly to its "shoulds."

On the other hand, narcissistic perfectionists have a poorly defined and weakly-differentiated self. Lacking a stable inner core, their sense of who they are is fragile, forcing them to rely on others' attention and admiration for their self-esteem. Like a barometer, this vulnerable self-esteem rises and falls, fluctuating between feelings of inferiority and superiority. When a significant person registers disapproval or criticism, narcissistic perfectionists feel defective; when praised or admired, they experience a grandiose or inflated sense of self. Instead of the guilt that neurotic perfectionists feel whenever they fail, narcissistic perfectionists experience the crippling shame that is symptomatic of early emotional wounding. The former are upset about *performing* badly, while the latter believe that they themselves *are* bad.

> ...the "tyranny of the shoulds" of the narcissistic perfectionist focuses on the self ("I should be perfect"). The failure to live up to the dictates of the "shoulds" evokes thoughts of "I am worthless," "I am a nobody" (shame). In contrast, the focal point of the neurotic individual's "should" is the action to be done or not done ("I should *never get angry*"). The failure to live up to this expectation evokes thoughts of "I am bad" (guilt).[13]

In short, narcissistic people are perfectionistic because their fragile self-esteem requires the reinforcing admiration of others. The very fabric of the narcissistic self is held together by perfection; thus failure is devastating. In contrast, neurotic perfectionism is related to morals and ideals. Neurotics slip into perfectionism because of their compulsion to obey the dictates of a demanding superego.[14]

PERFECTIONISM FROM A SPIRITUAL PERSPECTIVE

Perfectionism weakens the very foundation of our spiritual life because it impedes self-acceptance. Self-acceptance is foundational to faith because "sinful flight from God starts in one's flight from oneself."[15] Self-rejection easily leads to a rejection of God. When we are discontent with who and what we are, we cannot value our life as a worthwhile gift from a generous creator and so cannot respond to God with gratitude. At times, we may even feel resentment and bitterness, fueled by envious hatred of others, whom we perceive as having been dealt a better hand. Ingratitude results when our unique creation by God is not seen for the gracious act of divine love that it is. Struggling with an abiding sense that we are not enough, our perfectionistic self can slip into a self-hatred that not only blocks us from loving others but also alienates us from God.

Self-acceptance for Christians cannot be a selective process whereby some aspects of the self are claimed as good while others are discarded as undesirable. For self-rejecting perfectionists, the spiritual challenge is twofold. First, we need to embrace the fullness of who we are as persons uniquely fashioned by God. This means overcoming the tendency to selective self-acceptance. Second, we need to grow in a conviction based on faith that God's love for us is total and without regard for the flaws and limitations of which we are ashamed. Ultimately, spiritual growth occurs when we are graced with a felt-knowledge or emotional realization of our radical goodness and lovableness in the midst of our imperfection.

PERFECTIONISM AND PRIDE

The perfectionistic self easily falls prey to the sin of self-righteousness because unconsciously it seeks, Pharisee-like, to establish itself with God on the basis of its own achievements. In other words, we try to earn salvation through our good works rather than receiving salvation as an unearned gift. When tempted to gain God's favor through our own religious practice and works, we need to realize that we can never be more than creatures who are always in need of God's mercy and love. That these gifts are freely lavished on all by God is the essence of the good news preached by Jesus.

Perfectionistic pride also exposes itself in the harsh self-condemnation that follows when our performance fails to meet our unrealistic expectations. A study of first-year law students reported that eighty percent of them needed counseling for anxiety and depression.[16] The majority of these students exhibited perfectionistic tendencies that made them angry, depressed, frustrated, and panicky when they were not at the top or near the top of their class. Accustomed to being first in their undergraduate years, these high achievers were psychologically unprepared for the "average-student" role in which the more selective and competitive situation of law school placed them. Their perfectionism condemned them as second-rate or losers. This study illustrates how the excessively high standards of perfectionists can mask an implicit claim to superiority and an unwillingness to accept being "ordinary." In treating perfectionists who are heavily defended against recognizing this subtle form of pride, one psychologist recommends intervening with such statements as: "Holding such high standards is your way of saying, 'Nothing that I could ever do would be good enough for someone as superior as myself'"; or, "When you make a mistake, say to yourself 'I feel I am too good to make mistakes like other people.'" This form of intervention is based on the premise that seeing their self-condemnation as a fraudulent claim to superiority will give perfectionists a reason to stop it.[17]

"CHRISTIAN PERFECTION" AND SELF-ABSORPTION

The project of maintaining superiority in all things, combined with an obsession with mistakes, can so consume our attention and energy that we become narrowly focused on ourselves. Like a whirlpool, perfectionism sucks us into the hole of self-preoccupation. If we identify our worth with our performance, our activities become the mirror into which we gaze with narcissistic preoccupation, searching anxiously for reflections that will reassure us of our self-worth.

A self-absorbing pursuit of perfection has at times been fostered by a commonly misunderstood and misused exhortation of Jesus that as Christians we should "Be perfect as your heavenly Father is perfect" (Mt 5:48). Taken out of context, this passage has served as the basis on which Christians were urged to strive for individualistic moral perfection, to be flawless in thoughts, words, and deeds. If to be true followers of Christ necessitates embodying the perfection of God, it is no wonder that the pursuit of perfection has often resulted in fear, hypocrisy, and legalism.[18] Perfection, defined as being errorless, is a human impossibility. Yet it has masqueraded for centuries as the nature of true Christian holiness. When this biblical injunction is understood in its context, a very different image of "Christian perfection" emerges.

This well-known saying is taken from Matthew's sermon on the mount. It is immediately preceded by a description of God, who "makes the sun rise on the evil and the good" (5:45) and castigates those who love only people who love them. Thus, the context indicates that Jesus exhorts his followers "to imitate God by loving without distinction, not by becoming perfect paragons of virtue."[19] In other words, we are called to imitate the Father's indiscriminate and inclusive love, a love that causes him to let the sun rise on the bad as well as the good and to allow the rain to fall on the upright and the wicked alike. Thus, the passage is not advocating the pursuit of perfection as a striving for individual moral perfection, but rather a lifelong stretching of one's capacity to love as God does.

The Greek word used by Matthew for "perfect" is the term *teleios*. According to scripture scholar William Barclay, the term has nothing to do with what might be called abstract, philosophical, metaphysical perfection. Rather, a thing is *teleios* if it realizes the purpose for which it was planned or created. Matthew 5:48 makes clear that Christian holiness consists in being Godlike. And "the one thing which makes us like God is the love which never ceases to care for [people], no matter what [they] do.... We enter upon Christian perfection, when we learn to forgive as God forgives, and to love as God loves."[20]

When the focus of Christian holiness is kept on the ongoing development of the capacity to love as God does, the danger of self-absorption is minimized. When, however, the Christian ideal is seen as the perfect attainment of virtues, a radically different focus emerges. Concentrating on a life of faultless obedience and spotless virtue keeps us focused on our own scorecard of good works, rather than on the quality of our relationships. The life that the New Testament portrays as the proper response to God's generous gift of love is not a matter of pursuing individual excellence through perfect obedience, but a sincere imitation of Christ whose life centered on love and service of others. "Too often the pursuit of perfection," states contemporary moral theologian William Spohn, "becomes more concerned with the servant than with those who need to be served. In the New Testament, gratitude and compassion, not the drive for perfection, channel Christian commitment into action."[21]

Perfectionism and the Shadow

Striving for Christian perfection does not mean we must deny or reject any aspect of our personality. Nor does it legitimate the disowning of the shadow. Jung makes an important distinction between perfection and completeness: "One must bear in mind that there is a considerable difference between *perfection* and *completeness*.... The individual may strive after perfection...but must suffer from the opposite of his [or her] intentions for the sake of...

completeness."[22] The point here is that perfection belongs to God, while completeness or wholeness is all that human beings can hope for. Jung's thinking on this issue coincides with the gospel, because for Matthew, *teleios* does not mean being perfect, in the sense of being flawless, but rather moving toward the human goal of wholeness or completeness.

Embracing our existence as human beings is the way we become whole. One of the greatest challenges we will ever face is learning to appreciate our weaknesses and take ourselves less seriously. Life teaches us through our mistakes and failures. We learn humility and that we need the help of others. We learn to let others fail too. No longer demanding perfection of ourselves, we come to the joyful realization of our dependency on God and learn to trust that God's grace is enough. Confidence in God's unconditional love for us replaces our perfectionistic strivings with a peaceful acceptance of ourselves as we hear in the depths of our being the echo of the Zen master's words, "What you are is enough. What you have is enough."

Reflection Questions

1. How do you experience the symptoms of perfectionism in yourself and in others?

2. Discuss how perfectionism can impede spiritual growth and religious development.

3. The "Crock of Shoulds" Exercise.[23]

Purpose: First, to help a person to become more aware of the shoulds he or she is experiencing in the present; second, to recognize the source of these inner dictates; and third, to clarify how he or she wishes to respond to each of them.

Procedure:

1. Make a list of the shoulds you are experiencing in your life in the present. Make your statements brief and simple, expressing directly what you feel you ought to be doing and feeling without giving any reasons or explanations. Give life to your pen. Be as spontaneous as possible, trying not to filter or censor what automatically surfaces in your consciousness. Merely record what occurs at each moment.

Continue to list these "I shoulds" for ten to fifteen minutes. Write down whatever comes to mind, even if it means repeating yourself.

2. Look over the list and put a plus (+) next to the statements about which you feel positive, an "x" next to those about which you feel negative, and a question mark (?) next to those about which you have ambivalent feelings.

3. Try to identify the source of the shoulds that stir up negative feelings by asking "Where is this should coming from?" Can you associate any of these negative shoulds with a face or voice? Are these shoulds being imposed from someone in the environment or do they originate in yourself? Perhaps they originally came from someone in the environment, but have since been internalized to such a degree that it would be truer to say that the source is within yourself.

4. Once the source of the negative shoulds is identified, ask yourself how you want to respond to each at this time in your life. If the source is someone other than yourself, it could be someone close by, distant, or even dead (since death ends a life, not a relationship). Knowledge of the source will help you decide how you want to and can respond.

Comments on the Exercise

The value of this exercise is that it can clarify, for those driven or paralyzed by the tyrannical voices of inner shoulds, where the battle for freedom is to be fought—with someone in the environment or within oneself. If the source of shoulds is actually within oneself and being projected onto others, it would be fruitless and destructive to look for a solution outside oneself.

This exercise also helps a person to recognize shoulds that elicit positive feelings. Perhaps it would be more proper to label these as "wants" rather than "shoulds." Through this exercise, we can also examine those shoulds that stir up mixed feelings within us. By reflecting more concretely on our ambivalent reactions to these shoulds, we can gradually clarify our feelings and decide how we want to respond to them.

CHAPTER FIVE

ENVY:

A LONGING FOR WHOLENESS

It is from within, from our hearts, that evil intentions emerge: avarice, malice,
deceit, indecency, envy. All these
things come from within and make us
unclean.
MARK 7:21-23

ENVY IS AS COMMON as love or anger, and surely as powerful as any of
the passions of the human heart. Why, then, is it so rarely
acknowledged or discussed? Could it be because of its age-old
reputation for evil? Envy afflicts us all, at one time or another,
despite our best intentions and attempts to overcome it. While some
of us experience envy merely as an occasional and fleeting feeling,
others of us are "consumed by envy" and suffer gravely from the
psychic pain that results when envy dominates our lives and
consciousness.

FAMILIAR TALES OF ENVY

There are many literary works that portray the drama that envy can
create in human relationships. The biblical stories of Cain and Abel,
Joseph and his brothers, and the prodigal son, as well as the fairy
tale of Cinderella and Shakespeare's *Othello*, illustrate the destructive potential of envy and reflect its hateful intentions.

Cain, consumed with envy because Yahweh favored his brother,

78

Abel, was driven to fratricide (Gn 4:1-8). Joseph was the victim of his brothers' jealousy when they saw that "Israel loved Joseph more than all of his other sons...and came to hate him so much that they could not say a civil word to him" (Gn 37:3-4). However, Joseph's dreams foretelling a promising future in which he would rule over his brothers made the situation even worse. Joseph's dreams evoked his brothers' hatred and their jealousy then turned into murderous envy.

The elder brother in the parable of the prodigal son demonstrates how our perception that someone else is unfairly receiving more of "the good" than we are produces resentment and envy. In response to his father's plea for understanding, he, in a pout, complains: "Look, all these years I have slaved for you and never once disobeyed your orders, yet you never offered me so much as a kid for me to celebrate with my friends. But, for this son of yours, when he comes back after swallowing up your property—he and his women—you kill the calf we have been fattening" (Lk 15:29-30).

The fairy tale of Cinderella exemplifies another facet of envy: that someone's natural beauty and endowments can in themselves evoke envy in those who feel inferior. In this story, a beautiful young woman becomes the target of attack by her envious stepmother and stepsisters, who take delight in making her suffer.

Finally, Shakespeare lays bare the malicious destructiveness of envy in the character of Iago, the villain of the play *Othello*. Iago envies Othello's success and beautiful wife, Desdemona, and is driven to spoil Othello's happiness by conniving to make Othello suspicious of Desdemona's faithfulness. His scheme works and Othello becomes madly jealous of his loving wife and kills her. While Iago's envious behavior brought punishment on himself, it nevertheless succeeded in bringing ruin and tragedy to Othello as well. Even when the envious cannot gain what others possess, they seem set on depriving others of enjoyment.

Wherever envy surfaces, suffering is close by. In the words of Horace, "Sicilian tyrants never invented a greater torment than envy."[1] Generally speaking, it is we ourselves who suffer most from our envy. There is a masochistic quality to envy because envy produces more unnecessary pain to the envier than it does to the envied. An eighteenth century Jewish moralist makes this point well:

Envy is nothing but want of reason and foolishness, for the one who envies gains nothing for himself and deprives the one he envies of nothing. He only loses thereby.... There are those who are so foolish that if they perceive their neighbor to possess a certain good, they brood and worry and suffer to the point that their neighbor's good prevents them from enjoying their own.[2]

Yet it is undeniably true that our envy can also bring hurt and pain to others. The voice of envy can be like an inner tape convincing us that "anything I need will be withheld from me, so I will destroy the one who has what I lack." Thus, envy attempts to avenge itself by attacking those who innocently become its object. For both the envier and the envied, making sense out of this suffering is a painful challenge that often ends in defeat, leaving behind a confusion that is never resolved. Recognizing our envy and understanding its meaning can help us better cope whenever we feel the disruptive effects of envious feelings. Without this kind of awareness we easily fall victim to our own or others' envy.

ENVY AND THE SHADOW

Many of us fail to recognize our envy, so loath are we to admit to something that seems so demeaning. We treat envy as a poison that can be locked away in a cupboard, out of sight and out of reach where, we rationalize, it can do no harm. Perhaps this reflects the human tendency to hide the dark sides of ourselves, particularly those that make us feel small and ashamed. Because envy is one of the most difficult emotions to identify and integrate, it easily becomes part of the shadow, undermining our spiritual integrity. Christian theology and psychology both warn against minimalizing the potential destructiveness of envy. The Christian tradition, recognizing its inherent evil, ranks it as one of the seven deadly sins. Psychoanalysts also give a primary place to envy in analysis because they believe it underlies many of the problems in human relationships, causing rifts between spouses, siblings, friends, and nations.

As with any shadow problem, those who desire to grow spiritually must learn to recognize the many faces of envy. We must open ourselves to the frustrated longings that give rise to our envy, because hidden in our envy is a hunger for wholeness that has been thwarted. While each particular pang of envy has its own specific message, envy is essentially a hopeless longing for the fullness of life that God has promised to us as our birthright. Our ability to recognize its presence and decode its meaning can redirect this destructive emotion toward life-affirming goals. If we look closely at the emotion of envy, we discover two things. First, envy expresses both a deep longing for and a despair of ever receiving the good things of life. The envious person tries to take from others what he or she longs for. Second, envy is always found wherever gratitude is absent. While gratitude produces love, envy generates hate. Recognizing envy for what it is can be an opportunity for growth and healing.

ENVY VERSUS JEALOUSY

Jealousy and envy are often confused. Envy is the pain at seeing another have what I want for myself, whereas jealousy is the fear that I will lose what I have. The envious person, feeling angry when another person enjoys something desirable, wants to take it away or to spoil it. Jealousy, however, is mainly concerned with love. The jealous person fears losing a loved one to a rival. The root of the word "envy" is the Latin *invidere* or *invidia*, meaning "to look with malice or resentment...to begrudge." In other words, the envious person views things with "an evil eye." Webster's Dictionary defines envy as "a painful or resentful awareness of an advantage enjoyed by another joined with a desire to possess the same advantage." To this definition, psychologists add: "and the desire to destroy the one who is seen to possess the advantage." Envy is based on a belief that goodness is a limited commodity. If someone else has a lot of it, there is less for me. In short, jealousy differs from envy in that it involves a triangle in which one person is afraid of losing the affection of another to a rival. Envy, on the other hand, involves only two parties: one who feels envious and the other who is the object of the envy.

Jealousy refers to possessiveness of the other; envy to comparison of self with others. The example of a retreatant who shared his painful struggle with jealousy and envy clarifies how these two emotions differ. In a conversation with his director, he felt mortified to have to own up to these embarrassing feelings but realized that they were interfering with his ability to pray. Frustrated, he confessed that anger pervaded his life to the extent that he could not even go through the motions of prayer. And it was clear to him that jealousy and envy, like destructive arsonists, were responsible for fanning the flames of anger. So intense was his jealousy that the mere sight of his wife talking with another man could set him off. His possessive jealousy was driving their marriage to the brink of divorce. He was also tormented by envy. His continual comparison of himself with other men inevitably led to disquieting resentment. He resented their superior training and education, larger cars, better jobs, looks, skills, popularity, and so on. Because jealousy and envy were hindering his relationship with God and others, he needed to deal honestly with them in order to progress spiritually.

Comparing ourselves with others can trigger envy. The story of a middle-aged man illustrates how envious comparisons get stimulated.[3] Happily married to a woman with whom he felt physically and psychologically compatible, he was pleased with his college teaching job and his respectable, if modest, salary. He lived in a good neighborhood and his children benefited from quality public schools. Socially, he was satisfied with friendly colleagues and acquaintances, as well as with several close friends. All in all, he felt quite content about his life, that is, until he attended the twentieth reunion of his college graduating class.

Curiosity about how time and circumstances had treated his former classmates brought him to the event on campus. And curiosity quickly turned into envy when he discovered that many of his classmates had attained greater social, economic, and professional status than he had. Not only did they make more money and had what sounded like more exciting jobs, but also their children went to elite private schools and their wives seemed more educated and attractive than his.

The envious feelings stirred up by his discovery destroyed his contentment, and he returned home from the reunion disgruntled, feeling inferior and like a failure. No longer happy with his spouse, he resented her for not being more like the wives of his classmates. Whereas he was once satisfied with his position as a college professor, he now was dissatisfied with his modest income and the monotony and lack of influence of his job. He harbored a secret animosity toward his successful friends, as well as a barely conscious hope that some setback would befall them. In short, comparing himself with others at the reunion created an onslaught of envy and resulted in ongoing psychic pain that tainted the way he viewed his whole life. In the brief span of a weekend, envy clouded his perception and blinded him to the good that he once enjoyed in his life.

THE DYNAMICS OF ENVY

To fully understand the perplexing emotion of envy, we need to see how it stems from our human desire for fulfillment. Whenever we perceive something to be a good, we are attracted to it. We feel a desire to be close to it or to possess it. This happens whether "the good" is another person, a material object, a beauty of nature, or a valued trait such as happiness or generosity. Envy is intrinsically related to goodness. It stems from a deep longing for the good and a corresponding despair of attaining it. What we each come to value and desire as good is determined by our own unique personality. What is desirable to one person may not be so to another. Envy enters our hearts when we despair of ever receiving the good things we desire. Our sense of frustration and despair become fertile soil for envy, which flourishes wherever hope is lacking. Thus, we may keenly suffer when another succeeds, or take secret delight in another's failure.

Envy is the result of not appreciating the depths of desire that our human nature experiences. To be human is to have pockets of emptiness that endlessly hunger for fulfillment. St. Augustine's prayer, "You have made us for yourself, O God, and our hearts will remain restless until they rest in you," expresses the truth about our deep yearning, a yearning that leaves us feeling forever incomplete and pining for more. It is precisely this infinite dimension of our desires that keeps us longing for fulfillment. When we do not consciously embrace this aspect of our human condition, we become frustrated and envious. We forget that we are creatures destined to find completeness only in divine love. Envy makes us think that "if only I had such and such, I would finally feel complete." But eventually, as experience repeatedly bears out, disillusionment sets in and we come to hate the very thing we thought would satisfy us.

Instead of accepting limitation and loss as part of life, the envious think that others always have more and that no one ever gives to them. Envious people fixate so much on what others have that they fail to focus on what they themselves need and want. This lack of self-awareness impedes their taking responsibility for their own lives. Instead, they come to believe that others are to blame for what they are missing and get angry. Blaming others activates feelings of victimization and self-righteous revenge, causing them to want others to pay for making them feel so bad. What begins as their own suffering gradually becomes something that someone else has done to them. The emptiness and longing that they once felt are replaced by resentment and rage. And those who possess what they desire become the enemy whose happiness is at their expense.

ORIGINS IN EARLY LIFE

Like other human emotions, the capacity for envy is in everyone, but people's susceptibility to it varies greatly and is determined early in life. Envy is thought to have its roots in early childhood when, as helpless and dependent infants, we are at our neediest. Incapable of taking care of any of our own needs, we are most vulnerable to emotional and physical deprivation. Child psychoanalyst Melanie Klein believes that envy is born out of this total sense of dependency and that infants spontaneously feel envy toward the mother, whom they experience as all-powerful and able to give or withhold what they need.[4] Thus, Shakespeare's intuition has a psychological foundation when he states in *Romeo and Juliet* that a person can be stricken early

> As is the bud bit with an envious worm,
> Ere he can spread his sweet leaves to the air,
> Or dedicate his beauty to the sun.
> (Act 1, scene 1, line 156)

How envious we are as adults goes back to our experience of mother as giving or withholding. According to Klein, when the scale of need-satisfaction versus need-deprivation is tipped in the direction of satisfaction, the infant survives the envy stage with a healthy capacity to give and receive love. When the scale is tipped in the opposite way, due either to the insatiability of the infant's needs or to severe maternal deprivation, the child's predominant emotional experience is that of being empty rather than full. This experience, Klein believes, damages one's capacity to love. A sense of defeat and despair grows, eventually resulting in a personality that is prone to envy. Early in life, then, we learn through our experiences of need-satisfaction and need-deprivation either to appreciate the good or to hate it and attack those whom we perceive as possessing it.

DEFENSES AGAINST ENVY

Defense mechanisms, like denial and intellectualization, are unconscious ways of fending off painful feelings and avoiding unpleasant realities. Numerous defenses are used to cope with envy. In her classic work on envy, Klein suggests that there are so many as to make it impossible to list them all! These defenses serve to protect us from the painful exposure and retaliation we fear our envy will evoke. The most common of these are familiar to all of us, although we may not have thought of them as disguises for envy.

Idealization: Often we envy people we love and admire, especially when they seem to have and be all that we are not. Idealizing them and their gifts can be an attempt to lessen our envy. If the envy is very strong, however, this overvaluing may in time turn into hatred because it makes us feel inferior.

Devaluation: Devaluing is another way of warding off envy. Two common examples of devaluation are: the "sour-grapes" attitude that belittles what we have lost out on ("The prize wasn't that hot, anyway!") and the truism that "Rich people may have a lot of money, but money can't buy happiness." Once we have devalued something, our envious feelings seem to disappear. Devaluation inevitably happens to anything or anyone we idealize. Sooner or later our idealization gives way to disillusionment. How soon an idealization breaks down depends on the strength of the envy behind it. For some people, the tendency to spoil or devalue characterizes all their important relationships and they go from one relationship to the next, repeatedly disillusioned and disappointed.

Confusion: Inherent in envy is a sense of despair about ever attaining what we most desire. Overwhelmed by futility, we can experience great difficulty in making choices, both in weighty matters such as vocational and career decisions and in lesser matters such as what to select from a restaurant menu. The kind of indecision and unclear thinking that renders us incapable of arriving at conclusions is sometimes rooted in envious despair about ever getting what we want. The confusion that results in inactivity or procrastination wards off or defends us against envy.

Poor Self-Image: Devaluation of self or low self-esteem is another way in which envious feelings are avoided. This type of devaluing is most characteristic of people who are prone to depression. It may result in a lifelong inability to develop and successfully use our gifts, or it may arise only on certain occasions, as when there is danger of rivalry with an important person. The "payoff" for refusing to compete may be an avoidance of painful feelings of envy; the high price we pay for this escape, however, is the costly surrender of the chance to employ our gifts and to succeed.

Greed: Greed can be a subtle way of defending against envy. Envy, stemming from severe early childhood deprivation, leads to a neurotic inability ever to feel satisfied. Persons afflicted in such a way feel that "what I have and who I am is never enough." To compensate for this feeling, they may be driven to want or take all that they can get, whether in the form of material or spiritual goods. The greed that fuels insatiable acquisition allows one to be so preoccupied with "getting" and "getting ahead" that feelings of envy can be avoided. Perfectionism and professionalism can be manifestations of this tendency when they involve an endless pursuit of reassuring successes and achievements.

Making Others Envious: Stirring up envy in others by flaunting one's own success or possessions is a way of reversing the situation in which envy is experienced. The desire to make others envious and to triumph over them expresses both the hostility and the deep helplessness that characterize the inner world of the envious. An attitude of superiority or a tendency to brag about one's good fortune is a common mask for envy.

Hatred and Indifference: Another frequent defense against envy is stifling feelings of love and fueling feelings of hate. The envious person is confused by the mixture of love, hate, and envy that inevitably arises in close relationships and cannot tolerate the resulting ambivalence. One way to avoid this inner conflict is by denying the love. This may be expressed in either outright hatred or in an appearance of indifference. Withholding warmth and other manifestations of human kindness is a subtle form of revenge against those we envy.

Withdrawal: A variation of indifference is found in the allied defense of withdrawal from contact with others. Exaggerated self-reliance often masks a fear of envy and defends against it by avoiding experiences that will give rise to both envy and gratitude. The inability to ask for or receive help from others sometimes indicates a problem with envy, because excessive independence may be an envious refusal to acknowledge other people's strength.

Destructive Criticism: Malicious gossip, backbiting, and other forms of tearing people down are among the most common, everyday expressions of envy. The envious person feels unhappy at the sight of others' happiness and finds satisfaction and even joy in their misfortune. Discrediting or maligning the reputation of others is a widely recognized expression of envy.

VICTIMS OF ENVY

A professionally successful nun, who was an internationally known expert in her field, recounted the horror of being the scapegoated victim of her dysfunctional community. As a highly sought lecturer, she enjoyed all the "perks" that accompany such status. Since she found her work enjoyable but taxing, she was surprised to be the object of envy among the other sisters in the convent who unconsciously resented her freedom to travel ("her globe-trotting in the name of scholarship!"), while they felt tethered to a restrictive teaching schedule. What finally convinced her that envy was at the heart of the problem was the group's refusal to cooperate when a trained facilitator was brought in. No one would talk. After months of unsuccessful meetings, she realized that unconscious envy is impossible to deal with and asked for a transfer.

The above example illustrates how the envied person can be victimized. He or she feels attacked, threatened, and helpless. The envied may try to talk to the envier, to reason with him or her, even to try to prove that there is really nothing to be envied. As a last resort the envied may withdraw completely from any relationship with the envier. Victims of envy finally realize that there is nothing they can do to help the situation, because it is not a fault or a particular virtue that is provoking the hatred, but their very being.

Victims of envy may react with a variety of responses. If they feel angry about being persecuted, counterattack is the most likely reaction, and they become as destructive and hateful as the envier. Another response is to allow the envy to infect them. This happens if they internalize the blame projected on them and then feel guilty for being who they are. This was the case with a dynamic pastoral associate who was the unwitting victim of the envy of other staff members. Slowly he came to believe that he was as bad as his envious colleagues asserted. The result was a complete denial of the parts of his personality that had brought about their envy. Only after several years of therapy was he able to undo the damage and to regain the courage to be himself. His painful experience taught him what all of envy's victims need to realize: to capitulate to the envious perceptions of others is to betray valuable parts of oneself, even to jeopardize one's very sense of self. The temptation to abandon oneself is strongly felt by victims of envy, because of the suffering that this kind of persecution brings. Much courage is required to embrace the parts of oneself that trigger envy in others. Often it seems easier to disown or devalue one's talents or successes in an attempt to defuse the painful onslaughts of the envious.

ENVY IN GROUP LIFE

Special attention should be given to the effects of envy in group life, since most of us live and work in groups of one type or another. Experts in group dynamics commonly recognize that unconscious envy often lies at the heart of group conflicts. Seldom is a group created equal; inequality of natural gifts is inevitable. Such inequality, however, need not generate envy if the individuals are secure and confident enough to appreciate that each person has something valuable to offer. When this is the case, "We do not have to be or do it all. We can depend on others to supply what we lack," state Jungian analysts Ann and Barry Ulanov in their study of envy. We can, they add, "be glad for their abilities and talents, for together we make up a whole, and a desirable one."[5] However, when low self-esteem characterizes a group, we can expect that envy will rear its ugly head and be directed at any member who stands out because of some success or good fortune. Thus, celebrations of jubilees, weddings, anniversaries, and birthdays can occasion envious comparisons. Those who feel that no one ever gives to them or treats them as special may feel particularly resentful when others are honored.

Envy poisons group life. By polluting the atmosphere with their resentful feelings and undermining others' efforts to live and work cooperatively, envious individuals in a community have a negative influence on the whole group. They can sow seeds of dissension by secretly spreading rumors that foster mistrust, pitting people against each other and creating triangles.

Coping with the problems that come with group life requires more than faith and good intentions. If group members do not possess the skills for effective communication and conflict management, they will not be able to avoid the damage that envy can cause. Several envious people in a community can destroy the life of the whole group. A common way this occurs is through scapegoating: a few people consciously or unconsciously collude to designate one member as "the problem" and to convince the others of this. Systems theorists have demonstrated this dynamic quite convincingly in their work with families who have a "problem child." By treating the family group as a system, they are able to unearth the alliances and conflicts that exist in and among its members. By helping each family member learn how to communicate about his or her needs and feelings, they eliminate the need for a scapegoat.

Dysfunctional group norms, such as "being nice" and sweeping conflicts under the rug, pave the way for scapegoating by preventing members from voicing their feelings and airing their conflicts. An example of this occurred in a Christian community that resolved its unacknowledged conflicts by scapegoating a different person each year. On the surface there was a pretense of unity and cooperation. Those outside the group thought it a model community. The truth, however, was revealed not only in the scapegoating, but also in the group's inability to develop a meaningful prayer life and to communicate on more than a superficial level.

Envy in group life can show itself in less dramatic ways than scapegoating. Gossip, negativity (toward authority or peers who stand out in some way), and the withholding of affirmation and support are common ways in which group members can express their envy of each other. The inability to receive help from other group members or to express gratitude genuinely may also mask feelings of envy. Finally, envy in group life is sometimes reflected in the negative way that younger members may be treated by their elders. It is often painful for the aging to accept the increasing signs of their diminishment. Failure to embrace these inevitable losses creates resentment that drives a wedge of envy between the old and the young, preventing them from enjoying the good that they have to give each other. Some older people, feeling shortchanged, are intolerant of the young because the young enjoy what they never did. In family life, parents may find themselves having to deal with envious feelings toward their own children when they see them enjoying advantages that they themselves lacked when they were young. Paradoxically, parents can consciously want everything for their children and unconsciously begrudge them for having it so good.

RECLAIMING OUR LOST POTENTIAL

Envious persons refuse the call to actualize their God-given potential. Their preoccupation with what they do not have and their obsession with what others have blind them to what is their own. The unique gifts that are theirs go unrecognized and thus are lost to them. The very things that could give them substance and enhance their sense of being fall into the shadow, that psychic storehouse for all the disowned aspects of the personality. And because whatever is in the shadow gets projected onto others, the envious see their own neglected potentials reflected in those around them. This is why they resentfully believe that others have what belongs to them. Psychologically, it is true—not because others have taken it but because the envious person has unconsciously projected it onto them.

A couple of examples can help to illustrate the way in which this happens. A woman attending a faculty party with a friend finds herself feeling miserable as the evening progresses. She notices how relaxed and vivacious her friend is and how others naturally gravitate toward her. In contrast, she sees herself as a wallflower, self-consciously shy and fearful, and wishes she could be more spontaneous. Sometimes she resents her friend for always being the center of attention. She judges her as insensitive and selfish. But deep down, she knows the truth: she is envious and would give anything to be her! The moral of this story is not that the wallflower should try to imitate her extroverted friend, but that she needs to explore the unconscious fears that prevent her from moving out toward others as she secretly desires.

In other cases of envy, people find themselves obsessing over others' material possessions. A self-made businessman, for example, is envious of his neighbor, who owns a larger business and a new Mercedes. He feels inferior to his neighbor, whose wealth and power exceed his own. That he is a successful husband and father seems unimportant to him because he believes that a man's worth is measured by money and prestige. Because of the symbolic importance he has placed on these things in recent years, he has lost his appreciation of the family life that was once his first priority and source of happiness. That which formerly provided a sense of fulfillment and satisfaction has been lost. To overcome his envy, he would have to reclaim the inner values that are most important to him.

Envy can trap the envious in a vicious cycle because those around them unconsciously reinforce their low self-esteem. When we are with people who do not value themselves, we begin to devalue them too. Their self-deprecation not only colors our perception of them, it also makes them poor company. Their unhappiness may even make us feel guilty and apologetic, as if we have no right to be happy or take pride in our accomplishments. We may also find ourselves uncomfortable around them because we sense that they covet who we are and what we have.

ENVY AND THE SPIRITUAL LIFE

While psychology and literature offer valuable insights into the nature and dynamics of envy, a spiritual point of view offers some hope for the healing of envy. Looked at spiritually, envy represents a refusal to accept the human condition, particularly one's finiteness as a creature. Focusing on what others have that they lack, the envious betray themselves by preferring the being of others to their own. This refusal of the self "strikes a major blow against our spirit— that center of our integrity as unique and original persons. We are unwilling to take faith in that being which is ours...we flee it...[and] avoid thereby what we have been given, by focusing on what we lack."[6] While few of us find self-acceptance easy, the envier finds it impossible. The experience of being limited, of being imperfect and incomplete, is intolerable to the envious, who feel that they have nothing because they do not have everything. The spiritual failure of envy lies in the fact that self-rejection is also a rejection of God, who uniquely fashions each of us, right down to the number of hairs on our heads. As theologian Johannes Metz contends, "...self-acceptance is the basis of the Christian creed. Assent to God starts with [our] own sincere assent to [ourselves], just as sinful flight from God starts with [our] flight from [ourselves]."[7] Satan has been identified as the archetypal envier because he could not accept his rightful place in the order of creation. That he was not God was intolerable to him, so he turned against God, creating a kingdom of his own wherein he could reign. Milton makes this point in *Paradise Lost*, where he declares that envious rebellion entered the world through Satan:

> The infernal serpent; he it was, whose guile,
> Stirr'd up with envy and revenge, deceived
> The mother of mankind. (Book 1, line 34)

Envy also breeds sloth or laziness. In rejecting the being God has given them, enviers neglect the responsibility of developing their own gifts. Anyone who has spent years in developing a talent or honing a skill knows the discipline involved. To cultivate seriously our gifts and talents in preparation for a career that matches our potential requires hard work. Envy can prevent us from identifying and actualizing our own God-given potentials, which would bring us the sense of wholeness for which we long.

THE TRANSFORMATION OF ENVY

While it is important to analyze the psychological roots of envy, the healing of envy requires that we see its spiritual dimensions. At its core, envy harms our relationship to God as well as our relationship to ourselves and others. As a radical refusal to accept ourselves as we are, envy is sinful. Satan is the archetypal envier because he could not accept himself. Dissatisfied with his state, he allowed his envy to sever his relationship with God. Defying his creaturehood and striving for divine status created an attitude problem that he was unwilling to face and change.

The healing of envy requires a fundamental shift in attitude. First, envy must be seen for what it is—a sinful and spiritually destructive reality that calls for genuine conversion. Second, freedom from envy can come only when we recognize that as Christians we are meant to be always in longing until that day when God becomes our all in the heavenly Jerusalem. A holistic spirituality invites us to see the poverty that we experience as creatures, not as a negative void to be lamented but as a rich vacancy for God, who alone can satisfy our being. Third, concrete efforts must be made to examine the conditions that lead to envy. Only an awareness of how envy plays itself out in our personal life can bring about the capacity to escape its deleterious effects. For some of us what is needed is merely a redirection of our gaze to highlight the giftedness and goodness that we actually possess. Since envy is admiration turned sour, the solution to envy may be as simple as reawakening our capacity for wonder and appreciation. For others, however, whose envy is deep-seated and rooted in severe childhood deprivation, the help of a therapist may be required. Both the wallflower and the businessman mentioned earlier may eventually find themselves in this position. Like the woman in Luke's gospel who searches for a lost coin (15:8-10), they must have the determination to search actively within for what they have lost.

Envy can be a catalyst for transformation. When the needs and desires that it conceals are acknowledged, envy can point us in the direction of the good that we long for. Learning to detect in the swirl of envious feelings the precise need that longs for satisfaction is a critical step in discovering the grace hidden in the experience. Clear recognition of what it is that we need can direct our efforts in positive and constructive action. Envy is not something to be ashamed of, but rather a valuable message that should be heeded. Shame leads to denial, and denial obscures the message. When we can see our envy as a longing for wholeness, we can respond to ourselves with compassion and love. Forgiving our envy opens us to see the goodness that is ours. Thus the transformation of envy begins. Grace comes to us when we begin to appreciate the good that is already ours, even if what we possess does not include every possible good in human life. Then, we come alive to the fact that God has indeed been gracious to us. As our experience of the good expands, so will our sense of gratitude, and envy will start to shrink.

Since gratitude and envy are mutually exclusive, the way to heal an envious heart is to replace it with a grateful heart. This is one of the purposes of prayer, to remind us of the gracious generosity of God and to awaken in us a sense of appreciation for the goodness that is already ours. Prayer moves us deeply into the mystery of grace. In prayer, we open ourselves to the abundance of God; here our emptiness becomes a gift, rather than a curse, as God fills us with love. The more needy we are, the more we know our need for God. And in humility we begin to recognize the gifts and graces bestowed on us over our lifetime. Occasionally, when we least expect it, a grace we have long needed comes to us, and like C. S. Lewis, we are surprised by joy. Even our sufferings and losses become occasions of grace as we realize we were not abandoned, even when we abandoned ourselves. When gratitude becomes our way of life, we make peace with our envy, not excusing it or ignoring it, but acknowledging it as part of ourselves. Then, with the psalmist, we can pray: "It was you who created my inmost self, and put me together in my mother's womb; for all these mysteries I thank you: for the wonder of myself, for the wonder of your works" (Ps 139:13-14).

Reflection Questions

1. Recall times when you felt pleased when you heard of another's misfortune, or when you secretly rejoiced over another person's failure. Can you recognize how these were moments when you were experiencing envy? At each of these times, of whom and about what were you envious?

2. Have you ever experienced being the object of someone else's envy? Describe what occurred and how the situation was resolved. What in this chapter resonates with your experience? What does not?

3. Gratitude is the antidote to envy. When gratitude expands, envy shrinks. Make a personal litany of thanksgiving for all that you enjoy in your life.

CHAPTER SIX

OVERWORK:

A HINDRANCE TO WHOLENESS

We also witness the shadow in the workplace when people put aside their
personal needs for leisure, intimacy, and family, becoming around-the-clock
achievement machines.[1]
—Bruce Shackleton
"Meeting the Shadow at Work"

As a life-giving aspect of existence, human labor allows us to
embody our love for others with concrete acts of service, thus
enriching the life of families, communities, and nations. Satisfying
work also enhances our intellectual, psychological, and spiritual
development. As a contemporary writer puts it, "Take away the
opportunity to work, to create, or to care—as our society does to too
many people—and you have deprived someone of a chance to feel
fully human."[2] Work, done under humane and respectful conditions,
provides the human spirit an opportunity to express its creative
powers and to imitate its creator in whose image it was made.

But the shadow also shows up at work. Individual and collective
shadow problems often spoil the blessing that fulfilling work can be.
A Christian spirituality that honors the rightful place of work
requires valuing the contributions of work to human life, as well as
acknowledging its inherent limitations. Work cannot help but fail us
when we look to it alone to foster the wholeness that we seek. The
built-in limitations of any job render it incapable by itself of
satisfying all of our human longings. Thus, it is vitally important

that work not monopolize our lives, leaving no room for other human activities essential for holistic living and growth. Because work can lead to either personal wholeness or fragmentation, it has both "light" and "dark" sides.

MEETING THE SHADOW AT WORK

We encounter the shadow at work whenever we, in order to do our job, must deny important aspects of ourselves. Rigid role definitions and confining work patterns may force us to neglect or put aside certain personal values or beliefs. When successful role performance demands the sacrifice of our deeper humanity, we are experiencing the "dark side" of work. For example, a lawyer whose primary job is to challenge insurance claims may find that her compassion and empathy have no place in her workday if she wants to do a good job. In her work, only the hard-nosed succeed. Or a minister, in order to conform to the idealistic expectations of parishioners, may disown his own weaknesses and needs, in the name of doing a good job. The workplace contributes to "shadow making" whenever it causes us to "sell our souls to the company store," that is, abandon parts of ourselves in order to please others, whether they be bosses, colleagues, clients, or customers.

No matter the nature of our work, we inevitably cultivate certain skills and aptitudes while forsaking others in the shadow. As one writer expressed it, "If we cultivate an extroverted ambition, a powerful, competitive personality like a salesman, politician, or entrepreneur, our introversion goes into the shadow. We forget how to thrive outside of the limelight, receive riches from solitude, find hidden resources within. If, on the other hand, we develop a more private persona, as an artist or writer, our ambition and greed may go into the shadow, never to emerge, or one day to emerge suddenly like a ghost from a closet."[3] Clearly, we cannot expect to find either our wholeness or our fulfillment solely in our work.

WORK THAT DOESN'T WORK

When is work overwork? The problem of overwork arises when excessive and compulsive work robs us of the leisure we need for balanced living. "Feeling squeezed for time," "operating on overdrive," "getting by on five hours of sleep," "busy every waking hour" are common expressions that capture the condition of contemporary life in America for many people. We are experiencing "a crisis of leisure time," maintains Harvard economist Juliet Schor. In her 1991 study, *The Overworked American*, she highlights how overwork has become a national phenomenon. Ironically, even as many Americans suffer from both underemployment and unemployment, many others endure the pressure of working long hours and the subsequent decline of leisure.[4] According to Schor, "Nationwide, people report their leisure time has declined by as much as one- third since the early 1970s."[5] As a result, we are spending less time on such basic needs as sleeping and eating and devoting less attention to our children. The difficult balancing act of reconciling the demands of work and home life definitely increases stress. While the causes of child neglect, marital distress, sleep deprivation and stress-related illnesses such as ulcers, gastro-intestinal problems, backaches, and high blood pressure are complex, expanding work and shrinking leisure have clearly exacerbated each of these social ailments. Despite the oft-quoted motto that "No one ever died of hard work," overwork can cause death. In Japan, *keroshi*, or "death from overwork," typically affects men between the ages of forty and fifty who work twelve to sixteen hours a day. With no previous health problems, two-thirds of these men die of brain hemorrhages and one-third from myocardial infarction. These victims apparently just work themselves to death. Japan's Ministry of Health and Welfare reports that *keroshi* claims the lives of ten percent of working men in Japan and is the second largest killer of this population.[6]

But overwork destroys more than the body; it can also kill the spirit. Family and friends of workaholics frequently complain that overwork has transformed their loved ones into zombies, the "walking dead," who seem to have checked out of life. When we get preoccupied with our work, we cut ourselves off from relationships and become emotionally unavailable to others. Even more alarming, we abandon ourselves and lose touch with our own feelings, bodily needs, and inner life. Thus, overwork leads to fragmentation not wholeness, because it results in self-alienation, the condition of being a stranger to oneself.

There is nothing wrong with loving our work or with working hard. In fact, a certain sense of commitment to our work is essential if we are to be productive. Occasionally this commitment will mean that we have to work overtime to meet an important deadline or to respond to some unusual circumstance. The spiritual danger arises whenever our busyness, rushing and compulsiveness substitute for attending to the needs of our inner world. The compulsion to work seriously stifles the inner life of the spirit and undermines a holistic spirituality that seeks to deal with one's life in a balanced and adequate way, giving each significant aspect its due.

AWARENESS INCREASES PERSONAL "RESPONSE-ABILITY"

Individual differences make it necessary for each of us to examine our own situation to determine where things are out of kilter and adjustments need to be made. Not all of us are in need of the same thing nor is each of us endangered in the same way. A story, entitled "Monkey Salvation for a Fish," told by Anthony de Mello, nicely illustrates how vulnerability varies with individuals:

> "What on earth are you doing?" said I to the monkey when I saw him lift a fish from the water and place it on a tree.
> "I am saving it from drowning," was the reply.

To bring home the moral of this story, de Mello concludes, "The sun that gives sight to the eagle blinds the owl."[7] Thus, when addressing our patterns of overwork, we need to see what in our unique personality and peculiar background makes us vulnerable.

WHAT FUELS OVERWORK?

Only by understanding why we work as much as we do, and how the demands of work affect our life as a whole, can we hope to save ourselves from the physical and spiritual ills that overwork can wreak. The roots of workaholism, which are both psychological and social, are often hidden in the unconscious. Some of the factors that contribute to overwork are within our control and some are not. Awareness of those dynamics within our own personality that foster excessive work habits can increase our "response-ability" and thus increase our likelihood of achieving greater harmony and balance in our lives. Understanding the common causes of overwork can help us break its unhealthy grip on us.

Anxiety and Self-Esteem Issues: The relentless drive to work can stem from two forms of anxiety. One form, called "ontological anxiety," refers to the human vulnerability we all feel to known and unknown threats to our survival and well-being. It manifests itself, for example, in our fear of strangers, natural catastrophes, and life-threatening diseases. Another form of anxiety springs from insecurity about our own adequacy and lovableness as individuals. Both forms of anxiety can fuel overwork.

In response to ontological anxiety, we attempt to secure our lives by acquiring the power, self-sufficiency, and personal significance that can come through hard work. Amassing money and possessions, status, and power is a way to gain control and ward off ontological anxiety. Since no amount of money or power can ever guarantee our safety and protect us from the vicissitudes of life, we can never afford to rest. Here the shadow aspect that underlies our compulsion to work is basic insecurity. What is lost in our unconscious is the truth that we are utterly dependent as creatures on a transcendent Source for life and well-being. Until we accept our radical poverty as limited creatures, we will never be able to rely on the sustaining love of God, the source of our well-being and existence.

Anxiety stemming from feeling that we are not good enough also drives us to overwork. Like a nagging voice within, it demands that we compensate for our inadequacy, thereby proving our competence to ourselves and others, and gratifying our need for recognition. Fully functioning workaholics tend to judge themselves by their accomplishments; they feel compelled always to be doing something in order to feel good about themselves. This explains why we are often depressed by unfinished tasks or plagued by an inability to relax. When accomplishments are the measure of who we are, they become the focus of our lives. We must always be "getting things done." Experiences are valued insofar as they serve the purpose of work, not for their intrinsic worth. For example, socializing is not merely for the sake of friendship, but for networking; vacationing is not just for enjoyment and fun, but is the necessary "downtime" that precedes the lusty leap back to work. When work both grounds and justifies our existence, it is not difficult to understand how it can become such a consuming force in our lives. A wise old spiritual director once summarized the danger of making work the raison d'être of one's existence when he said, "If you *are* your work, when you're not working, you *aren't*."

Affirmation-Deprivation and Self-Doubt: Many of us overextend ourselves when we work in "affirmation deserts," environments that do not nourish us with regular appreciation or positive feedback. In these settings, self-doubt can trigger frenzied attempts to capture people's attention and affirmation ("I'll prove it to them!"). When the desired affirmation does not follow, however, we, in our disillusionment and exhaustion, feel resentful (for being neglected), apathetic ("So, who cares? Why kill myself for nothing?"), and inadequate ("I really am a loser," or "I'll never be good enough"). Unmitigated by positive feedback from others, severe self-doubt can lead to discouragement and paralysis ("I don't have what it takes; I quit!").

Fleeing the Self: People with poor self-esteem often avoid getting to know themselves. They fear that there may be no one inside worth knowing, that the void within is an emptiness too fearful to explore. In this case, compulsive overwork can be a defense against facing oneself as well as a way of concealing one's shameful inadequacy from others. Keeping busy wards off painful encounters with the self and with others.

Dulling Painful Reality: Related to this avoidance through hyper-activity is the use of work as a narcotic to anesthetize inner turmoil. Work numbs the anguish of unresolved pain and also serves as a convenient excuse to escape from dealing directly with interpersonal conflicts. Workaholics are afraid that if they stopped long enough to listen, they might feel emotions that they wish to avoid. By overscheduling themselves, they continually operate in emergency mode, allowing the uproar of crisis to drown out their true emotions. In this way, work effectively stifles unwanted feelings and keeps them inaccessible.

Busyness as a Badge of Honor: Being busy is a common way we unconsciously promote our significance. In his book *The Client*, novelist John Grisham vividly illustrates how overwork is worn as a badge of importance and status:

> "Have a seat," Foltrigg [U.S. Attorney for the Southern District of Louisiana] said, pointing at a chair. "We're finishing up." He stretched too, then cracked his knuckles. He loved his reputation as a workaholic, a man of importance unafraid of painful hours, a family man whose calling went beyond wife and kids. The job meant everything. His client was the United States of America.

Trumann [FBI agent in New Orleans] had heard this eighteen-hour-a-day crap for seven years now. It was Foltrigg's favorite subject—talking about himself and the hours at the office and the body that needed no sleep. Lawyers wear their loss of sleep like a badge of honor. Real macho machines grinding it out around the clock.[8]

A relentlessly demanding schedule can reassure us, like certificates and diplomas on an office wall, that we are indeed important people caught up daily in the sweep of significant events!

Addiction to Being Busy: Being busy can also reach a point where it is an addiction. Some people report that they are hooked on the adrenaline high that comes with pushing themselves so hard. They have become addicted to the high of living life in the fast lane, moving on overdrive. Thus, they maintain a grueling schedule, filled with a never-ending series of urgent projects. Whenever one task is accomplished, there is something else equally urgent that must get done. The push to keep going is both an attempt to sustain the adrenaline high and a way of defending against the depression that inevitably descends when there is no work to do.

A "Positive" Addiction and a Pseudo-Virtue

Despite its harmful effects on personal and family life, overwork often masquerades as a virtue and finds its deceptive disguise safeguarded by both cultural and religious beliefs. In America, to argue that overwork is an obstacle to wholesome growth and spiritual development is to criticize a sacred cow. Culturally, there is a strong predisposition for hard work, which is promoted as productive and beneficial to society. The idea that Americans are obsessed with work is reflected historically in a Massachusetts law passed in 1648 that made idleness a punishable crime. A contemporary historian asserts that "the elevation of work over leisure" is an ethos that has "permeated life and manners" in our nation.[9] Consequently, it is not surprising to hear people brag about how hard they work and to regard their compulsion to work as a "positive addiction."

Religiously, overwork finds justification in an ethic that identifies personal achievements as proof of God's favor and in the fear that "idleness is the devil's workshop." For many Christians, the word "leisure" spontaneously elicits feelings of discomfort and guilt. Many of us claim that we have been conditioned from childhood to associate leisure with "being lazy," "wasting time," "useless," "being selfish," and "lacking apostolic zeal and generosity for service." Ministers, priests, and religious have been taught that their motto in ministry should always be, in the words of a well-known prayer for generosity, "to give and not to count the cost, to toil and not to seek for rest."[10] When applied without prudence and common sense, this lofty ideal has seriously affected men and women religious to the extent that many feel incapable of relaxing and at the same time have a nagging feeling that whatever they do is never enough.

St. Ignatius' observation in his *Spiritual Exercises* about how good Christians are tempted helps us to recognize overwork for the pseudo-virtue that it is. According to him, people striving to do good are tempted, not by gross evil, but by subtle evil camouflaged under the guise of good. He warns that what initially glitters like gold may end up as fool's gold. At first, overwork appears to be a sensible expression of generosity and dedication; but when it ends in joyless exhaustion, leading to the deterioration of prayer and personal relationships, it exposes its true nature as an obstacle to wholeness and holiness. Unfortunately, many sincere people confuse goodness with meeting the expectations of others, whether these match inner capabilities or not. Organizational consultant Diane Fassel reports her experience of how overwork and the neglect of leisure have exacted a heavy toll on Protestant ministers:

> I am in Iowa, at a convention of Protestant ministers from around the state. They are ruddy, hardy, hard-working people, mostly ministering in rural communities. The ministers come from farm families, where the motto is, "No one ever died of hard work." They believe this statement, for their experience is that hard work keeps you out of trouble and makes a positive contribution to family and community. Unfortunately, something new is happening in rural Iowa. Young and middle-aged ministers are leaving the ministry—disillusioned and unhappy. Working harder doesn't seem to help. They are burned out on caring.[11]

Denying the Problem

Workaholism is one of the few addictions people brag about. When it comes to overwork, denial looms large. It is difficult for many of us to admit that overwork is a problem, even when we and those who share our lives feel its painful effects daily. The work addict's denial has several dimensions. Some workaholics deny their problem by using the ploy of comparison. While admitting that they are compulsive workers, they nevertheless insist that overworking is better than a lot of other things they could be doing. Others deny their workaholism by highlighting the benefits they receive as a result of their industriousness. In their minds, these benefits make up for whatever cost their overwork may exact. For them, it is a worthwhile trade-off. Finally, some admit their addiction to action, but deny that it is damaging them in any way. These and other forms of denial are reinforced when they receive the support of codependent family and friends, who both benefit and suffer from their relationship to a workaholic. As Fassel puts it, these codependents "mimic the denial of the workaholic in their own complaints: 'He's a great provider, but we never see him'; or 'I suppose she could be doing worse things than working all the time, like running around with other men,' or this line from a Glasbergen cartoon, 'Do you have any perfume that smells like a desk? My husband is a workaholic.'"[12]

Whatever form it takes, denial does little to improve our lives; only a humble admission of our struggle with overwork and honest soul-searching of our unconscious motives can transform a life characterized by compulsion into a life of choice and freedom.

Perfectionism and Overwork

Compulsive overwork and perfectionism often go hand in hand. The desperate need to get everything done exactly right is a cruel tyrant that mercilessly drives some people to perpetual overwork. Despite the stereotype of workaholics as high-powered executives and fast-track professionals, one does not have to be in the corporate world to be afflicted with compulsive overwork. Women, for example, whose identity and worth hinge on being perfect wives and mothers, are just as liable to being consumed by work. To strive to be a "Super Mom" today is to flirt with overwork, because contemporary "standards have crept up for nearly everything housewives do—

laundry, cooking, care of children, shopping, care of the sick, cleaning."[13] Despite the introduction of labor-saving innovations—vacuum cleaners, washing machines, microwaves, ready-made clothes, and processed food—no labor has actually been saved, because modern standards of household cleanliness have escalated. Housework has expanded to fill the available time to do it.

The problem of perfectionism has been treated separately in Chapter Four, but the following examples illustrate the relationship between perfectionism and overwork. A student pursuing a graduate degree in English related that she had a weekly essay due for a literature seminar that met on Friday afternoons. After devoting the entire weekend to the required reading and study, she would start writing the essay on Monday morning and finish it by Wednesday night. Completing the essay by Wednesday should have given her time to devote to her other assignments. However, she found herself using the extra two days before the deadline obsessing over what she had done, endlessly reworking and revising her paper until it was "perfect." By the time she got to her Friday afternoon seminar, she was not only exhausted, but also behind in her work for other courses and feeling the pressure of having to catch up. This nerve-racking cycle was repeated weekly. Despite the negative toll it was having on her physically and emotionally, her perfectionism was so ingrained that she felt unable to curb her destructive work pattern. Professional counseling later enabled her to understand the psychological roots of her perfectionism and gave her some power over her compulsive overwork.[14]

The story of a married deacon hovering on the brink of burnout further illustrates how overwork and perfectionism interact. The deacon functioned successfully for many years as a pastoral associate in a busy urban parish. From the start, he realized that the opportunities for serving were boundless and he felt compelled to do as much as he could. The open-ended nature of his ministry was fertile ground for overwork. Despite long hours, he felt guilty whenever things were left undone. His idealism and diverse talents, as well as the overwhelmingly positive response of parishioners, sustained his initial years of ministering on overdrive. But the situation finally came to a head when he arrived at a retreat with the symptoms of burnout: exhausted, depressed, disillusioned, resentful, discouraged, and confused. While relating his condition to his retreat director, he had a flash of insight that brought grateful tears to his eyes because it promised the possibility of release from his bondage to work. For the first time, he was able to link his overwork to a need for approval and praise in order to bolster a weak sense of self. He suddenly realized that his drivenness was fueled by an unconscious desire to gain the affirmation of the elderly pastor; it was a way of winning from a father-figure the paternal approval he deeply craved and never received, because his own father had abandoned his family when he was only five. Even though he realized that much inner work and prayer would have to follow before his workaholic pattern could be reversed, this graced insight was the beginning of a long process of healing.

THE MESSIAH COMPLEX

An unconscious messianic complex frequently snags people into the trap of overwork by fostering the illusion that "everything depends on me." Psychotherapist Carmen Berry describes the "messiah trap," as a "two-sided lie that, taken at face value, appears to be noble and godly and gracious."[15] Side one is "If I don't do it, it won't get done" and side two is "Everyone else's needs take priority over mine." This two-sided lie reflects the grandiosity that characterizes compulsive overworkers, who have an exaggerated sense of both their own abilities and the importance of their projects. This inflated sense of self-importance deludes them into thinking that they are indispensable and therefore must be on the job twenty-four hours a day. Modern day messiahs exhibit a certain pride and condescension when they deny their own needs and limits and elevate themselves above the human condition. One sure sign that we have fallen into the messiah trap is when we find that we are quick to give but loath to receive.

The story of a middle-aged minister illustrates how a messianic mentality can affect one's choices. Having served successfully the poor and downtrodden for many hard years, he was given a sabbatical for rest and renewal. In the course of his year off, he spent some time at a spirituality center learning the art of spiritual direction. Surprisingly, he discovered a deep desire to include spiritual direction as part of his future ministry. This attraction to a ministry devoted to nurturing the spiritual growth of others was also seen as an invitation to better integrate his own *anima*, the feminine side of his personality. Although such a ministry was in stark contrast to his prior work as a social activist, he experienced it as a call from God, a religious inspiration that needed to be reverenced and honored.

Upon returning home, he faced a number of options for work: some with the possibility of doing spiritual direction and others that would leave no room for it. Among these choices, one had an urgent appeal to him. It involved working in an inner-city parish that was engulfed in crisis and floundering badly. He was deeply conflicted. At times, he felt the urge to rescue a faltering operation, even though the inner-city work threatened to be all-consuming, leaving no time to do spiritual direction. At other times, he vigorously resisted the notion of abandoning his newly-felt call to a ministry dedicated to the spiritual development of individuals.

In the course of his discernment process, he had a dream that confronted him with his tendency to toss aside important personal needs whenever a desperate situation activated his messianic instinct. Prior to going to bed, he was in his office distributing the personal effects of a deceased colleague and close friend who was highly esteemed by the parishioners. He freely gave whatever each parishioner requested, thinking to himself: "That's me. Whatever people want from me, they can have." Later that night, he dreamed that a woman secretary was handing out the personal effects of his deceased colleague. When she got to a statue of the Blessed Virgin Mary, she exclaimed, "No, you can't have this. I need this."

Like the dream that directed the three magi to avoid King Herod on their return home, the minister's dream also bore wise guidance. It was the psyche's attempt to restore balance to a conscious identity that was out of touch with its own neediness and unable to lay legitimate claim to what is required for survival and growth. The dream had a compensatory function in that it evened out a one-sidedness in his thinking. When he applied its message to his discernment, he felt he was being cautioned against an impulsive suppression of his desire to do spiritual direction, which would also mean abandoning his *anima*, symbolized in the dream by both the woman secretary and the statue of the Virgin. The dream, like a wise nocturnal counselor, reminded him that there are certain values to which he must cling for the sake of wholeness. It also illustrates the shadow side of the messianic complex which obscures our own vulnerability and need to be saved.

CODEPENDENCY AND OVERWORK

While Chapter Three gives a comprehensive treatment of the psychological roots and dynamics of codependency, the issue of codependency is mentioned here because of its relevance to overwork. Having much in common with the messiah trap, code-pendency is a form of compulsive helping that is motivated by the need to be needed. Like those ruled by the messianic complex, codependents thrive on being needed by others. They too help others at grave cost to themselves because of unhealthy attitudes about self-care: "It's selfish to consider my own well-being"; "I shouldn't pay attention to my own needs"; "Never say no to a request for help." In short, legitimate self-care languishes in the shadow like some forgotten prisoner in an overcrowded foreign jail. What distinguishes a messiah complex from codependency? The former's plight stems from an inflated sense of self, while the latter's condition is the result of an addiction to relationships. For example, an unconscious grandiosity seems to characterize fanatic social activists who are absolutely convinced that they alone, like latter-day messiahs, hold the key to solving the world's problems. They seem always to be consumed in a cause that will finally bring happiness and peace to the planet. Codependents, on the other hand, are inordinately attached to relationships and overwork because of their fear that saying "no" will disappoint others and incur their disapproval.

PRESSURE TO PRODUCE

External pressures, whether social or economic, can also contribute to overwork. Social pressure often comes from organizations with grandiose goals. These "addictive" organizations create expecta-tions and demands that cannot be fulfilled, and the attempt to do so can hurt the well-being of the workers involved.[16] Many church and humanitarian groups fall into this category. Furthermore, it has been observed that it is the most codependent-prone members of such dysfunctional systems who feel responsible to fulfill these unrealistic goals, often to their own detriment. It is no wonder that so many ministers and church workers complain about the pressures of work and worry about burnout. Church-related organizations that care more about their grandiose goals than about the human needs of their members develop the same collective shadow problems as any big business. They become impersonal and inhuman.

Economic pressure is created by workaholics who often set the standards for job retention, salary increase, and promotion—standards to which others feel constrained to comply, whether they like it or not. As long as there are a few workaholics around, competition and human respect build up the pressure on others to keep up. Because employers prefer "dedicated" workers, rewarding them with promotion and praise, workaholics have an advantage over those who for reasons of personal preference or competing family duties do not put in the long hours. Thus, workaholics up the ante, setting a pace that others feel constrained to follow as a matter of sheer economic survival.

THE COLLECTIVE SHADOW OF WORK: VALUING PROFIT OVER PERSONS

Because it is more profitable for employers to put workers on overtime than to train and provide benefit coverage to new employees, even people who want less work and more leisure may not have that option. In America, productivity, which measures the amount of goods and services that result from each hour worked, has grown. With the growth of productivity, laborers can either produce the current output in less time or work the same number of hours and produce more. Theoretically, increased productivity presents the possibility of either enjoying more free time or making more money. This is what economists call the "productivity dividend." In reality, however, workers seldom have the chance to exercise an actual choice about how they make use of their productivity dividend, because, as Schor observes, "with few exceptions, employers (sellers) don't offer the chance to trade off income gains for a shorter work day or the occasional sabbatical. They just pass on income, in the form of annual pay raises or bonuses, or, if granting increased vacation or personal days, usually do so unilaterally."[17] For instance, a single-parent recently made a career switch from teaching to financial consulting so that she could better provide for her children. In her first year in the field, she made more money than she had teaching and was the top earner in the firm. Since her earnings were adequate for her family's needs, she told her manager that she would prefer less working hours and more time at home. Her manager responded with the requirement that she increase her production by twenty-five percent.[18]

CAPTIVES OF CONSUMERISM

Since the 1930s, the choice between work and leisure, contends Schor, has hardly been a choice at all, at least in any conscious sense, because Americans have drifted into a pattern of consumption, a "work and spend" cycle, that has become a powerful dynamic keeping them from a more relaxed and leisured way of life.[19] Once considered a necessary chore, shopping has become a national passion and "malling" a popular form of weekend entertainment. While consumerism is mainly an affliction suffered by the affluent and the middle class, even the poor are captivated by the dream, fed by slick and subtle television commercials, of better living through the acquisition of more and better possessions. "The poor are not so much adherents to an alternate (antimaterialistic) set of values as they are unsuccessful at the same game everyone else is playing."[20]

The belief that "more is better" pressures us to work harder and longer just to make ends meet. As the cost of living increases so do our work hours. At its severest form, this belief results in an addiction that drags victims to the doors of self-help groups like Debtors Anonymous and Shopaholics Limited, acknowledging that they have lost control over their lives. The tendency to consume beyond need is abetted by the ease of buying "on time" and "enabled" by plastic. It is further fueled by advertisers whose livelihood depends on creating and expanding "needs." Advertisements aim to convince us that what we have is not enough and that happiness is just one more purchase away. Manufacturers, too, fuel our discontent with a strategy of planned obsolescence and continual upgrades for existing equipment. As long as consumerism runs rampant, the burden of overwork and the decline of leisure will continue in American life. Deliberation and conscious choice are critical if we are to escape the "squirrel's cage" of overwork and reclaim leisure.

Understanding some of the psychological and cultural underpinnings of consumerism can help us curb its course. At its core, consumerism's magical spell over us relies on the hopes and expectations we place on consumer products. Name-brands and designer-labels, for instance, are purchased with the hope that they will increase our self-esteem and raise our social status. The latest fashions promise to make us attractive and appealing, thus playing on our unmet needs to be loved. Advertisers promise that their products will fill the voids in our lives, fulfilling not only our physical needs but also our emotional longings. These subliminal messages are so effective that "many couples concentrate on owning a house or filling it with nice furnishings, when what they really crave is an emotional construction—home."[21] In a consumer society, material goods are also called upon to serve as reassurances of love and care, as when absent parents attempt to assuage their children's feelings of abandonment (and their own guilt) by indulging them with every imaginable toy or game. The psychology behind promotion and advertising is so effective that intelligent, rational adults will go into debt, spending the limit on several credit cards at a time, so that they can fulfill their loved ones' every material desire. Unfortunately, everyone pays the price for this kind of overspending—those who must overwork to keep creditors at bay, and their loved ones who feel cheated and bereft of a spouse or parent who is never at home.

"DUE TO CIRCUMSTANCES BEYOND OUR CONTROL..."

When tackling the stressful problem of overwork in our lives, the "Serenity Prayer" of Alcoholics Anonymous provides an important perspective. In that prayer, one asks God for the serenity to accept what one cannot change, the courage to change what can be changed, and the wisdom to know the difference. By looking realistically at our concrete situation, we can distinguish between what can and what cannot be changed in our life situation. There are certain economic realities that set limits on our choices. For example, some people need to hold down two or three low-paying jobs just to make ends meet.[22] Working women are also prime victims of the shortage of time when they are forced to cope with the demands of both wage work and housework, not to mention, in many cases, childcare. It is not, then, surprising to hear working mothers describe themselves as "ragged," "bone-weary," and "overwhelmed," since they effectively hold down two full-time jobs and find themselves in perpetual motion as housewives and mothers. Contrary to what might be expected, the rise of women's working hours has not resulted in their husbands' spending less time on the job. As working men also put in longer hours, the "5:00 dads" (who are able to be home for dinner and an evening with the family) are an endangered species. With the rising cost of supporting and educating children, many parents understandably find overtime or moonlighting financially compelling. As the "Serenity Prayer" exhorts, where there is no choice, we must peacefully accept our situation; but where there is choice and possibility of change, we need the courage to do whatever is necessary to restore balance to our hectic lives.

BALANCING WORK AND LEISURE

Balance is the key to a spiritually vibrant life. A story about St. Antony (251-356), one of the great wisdom figures of the Desert tradition in Egypt, Syria, and Palestine, illustrates how the saint recognized the importance of balancing work with leisure.

> Once the great Antony of the Desert was relaxing with his disciples outside his hut when a hunter came by. The hunter was surprised to see Antony relaxing, and rebuffed him for taking it easy. It was not his idea of what a holy monk should be doing.
>
> Antony replied, "Bend your bow and shoot an arrow."
>
> And the hunter did so.
>
> "Bend it again and shoot another arrow," said Antony.
>
> The hunter did so, again and again.
>
> The hunter finally said, "Abba Antony, if I keep my bow always stretched, it will break."
>
> "So it is with the monk," replied Antony. "If we push ourselves beyond measure, we will break. It is right from time to time to relax our efforts."[23]

A healthy spiritual life requires that we strike a balance between and among our various obligations and personal needs. Christians who follow the way of Jesus can find in his life a rhythm of holiness that included time for ministry, for withdrawal, and for relaxing in the congenial company of friends. Even in the midst of a demanding public ministry, he had a mountaintop, a desert place, a chosen few, dinner companions, and conversation partners.

BEING KEPT BY THE SABBATH

No life should be so busy with work that it excludes time for prayer and friendship, for leisure and solitude, for play and humor. And no work should be so all-consuming that there is no time to take stock of it; no schedule so tight that there is no room to reflect on whether what is being done is worth the doing. Hence the importance of honoring the sabbath and fostering a "sabbath-sense" in our lives. The sabbath, according to scholars of the Talmud, is greatly emphasized in Genesis to show that God created rest and commanded it of us. The sabbath-rest, the rabbis insisted, was vital to creation for three reasons. First, it equalized the rich and the poor, since on at least one day of the week, rich and poor were equally free from the constraints of work. Second, the sabbath provided time to evaluate our work—as Yahweh had evaluated the work of creation—to determine whether our work, like God's, was good. And, finally, the purpose of the sabbath, the rabbis declared, was to give us time to contemplate the meaning of life.[24] For all three purposes, observing the sabbath is critically important today, especially in light of the dangers of overwork and work addiction described in this chapter.

The sabbath is more richly understood, not as a date, but as an atmosphere. The sixteenth century Jewish rabbis known as the Safed Kabbalists used to speak about receiving the "sabbath-soul." On the sabbath, a different spirit holds sway than on the other days of the week. There is a different climate and mood. The ancient rabbis stated that as the Jew enters into the sabbath, the sabbath enters into the Jew. So important to the vitality of life was the sabbath that this was said of it: "More than the Jews kept the sabbath, the sabbath kept them."[25] Strong is the temptation today to lose ourselves in work in order to buttress a shaky self-esteem, to escape lonely and painful reality, and to seek happiness in the glow that comes with a spending spree or an adrenaline high stoked by fast-paced action. Perhaps more than our predecessors on this planet, we badly need the sabbath to keep us.

Reflection Questions

1. In what ways does your work contribute to your wholeness and growth? In what ways is your work an obstacle to a balanced life and spirituality?

2. Review the different factors that can fuel overwork. How have you observed these factors at work in yourself and in others?

3. What is the place of leisure in your life? What have you found to be fruitful and enjoyable ways of spending your leisure time? What have you found to be unsatisfying?

CHAPTER SEVEN

INTIMACY:

A CRUCIBLE OF WHOLENESS

For one human being to love another:
that is perhaps the most difficult of all our tasks, the ultimate, the last test and
proof, the work for which all other work is but preparation.[1]
—Rainer Maria Rilke
LETTERS TO A YOUNG POET

IT IS IN THE ARENA of relationships that our needs for self-knowledge and self-transcendence come together. We cannot even enter into relationship with another person unless we have some sense of self-awareness and at least a minimal ability to be concerned for another. In close, intimate relationships the best and worst in us are brought to the fore, providing us with a unique opportunity for transformation in the give-and-take that such encounters involve. Love relationships and other forms of commitment force us to grow up, challenging us where we are stuck in old but familiar self-images and patterns of self-centeredness. Intimacy brings us face-to-face with those shadow parts of ourselves that we tend to deny and project onto others, revealing to us "that which we have no wish to be." When intimacy is accompanied by love, it can become a crucible for our wholeness, stirring up what needs to be integrated and holding us in love as we meet those parts of ourselves which we have feared and hated.

INTIMACY: THE HEART OF CHRISTIAN LIFE

Intimacy is the hallmark of the Christian life. The most outstanding feature of Jesus' relationship with God was its intimate nature. Radically departing from Jewish tradition, Jesus incensed the religious leaders of his time by daring to address God as "Abba," an Aramaic term for "father" with all the familiarity and closeness that the term "daddy" or "papa" connotes today. Jesus' parable of the prodigal son proclaims the good news that God's way of loving is lavish and forgiving. Like the righteous older son in the parable, we struggle to understand a love that is so utterly without conditions, a love without any "ifs" and "buts." Jesus' intimate knowledge of God is repeatedly revealed throughout the gospels as he invites us to share in this same life of intimacy, which is the kingdom of God. That we have been made for intimacy is something our hearts intuit; that God is the source and fulfillment of our longing for intimacy is what Jesus proclaimed.

The gospel of John contains a helpful and concise biblical summary of the Christian belief that intimacy is the core of Christian life. In the context of his farewell discourse, Jesus says to his disciples: "As the Father has loved me, so I have loved you.... Love one another as I have loved you" (15:9, 12). This new commandment that Jesus handed down to his disciples right before his death epitomizes his total message. As Christians we are called to experience ourselves as the beloved of God and to embrace others just as we ourselves have been so intimately embraced by God. To reinforce his words, the author of the fourth gospel presents two scenes of intimacy that concretely illustrate what this commandment of love entails. Both scenes depict two persons intimately juxtaposed to each other, with one of the parties resting in the "bosom" of the other. The Greek word *kolpos*, meaning "bosom," found only twice in John's gospel, connotes affection, according to scripture scholar Raymond Brown.[2] The first time the term appears is at the end of the prologue in chapter one: "No one has ever seen God; it is the only Son, who is nearest to the Father's heart (*kolpos*), who has made him known" (1:18). In this scene of intimacy, it is Jesus who is affectionately nestled in the bosom of God. The only other time the term is used in the gospel is in the passage describing the last supper. Once again, we see a person resting closely to someone, with his head in the *kolpos* of another. This time, it is the "disciple whom Jesus loved" reclining at the table with his head in the *kolpos* of Jesus (13:23-26). Besides designating a particular historical figure who was close to Jesus and who shared in the last supper, the appellation, "the disciple whom Jesus loved," is also meant to symbolize and include all Christians who have a common call to intimacy with Jesus.[3] These two scenes of people in intimate juxtaposition are pictorial parallels of what the author states in prose: "As the Father has loved me" is captured in the scene of the preexistent Son in the *kolpos* of the Father; "so I have loved you" is visually expressed by the scene of the beloved disciple with his head in Jesus' bosom at the last supper. While these Johannine passages image God as Father, the underlying message is that each of us is meant to rest intimately in the *kolpos* of God, whether we image the divine as father or mother. Furthermore, Jesus' commandment to "love one another as I have loved you" calls us to allow others to draw close to us in intimacy, to rest in the affection and warmth of our hearts.

INTIMACY AND CHRISTIAN HOLINESS

When we speak of the need for intimacy what we mean is simply the need for close personal relationships. According to psychologist Erik Erikson, intimacy is an important developmental task that requires the ability to both sacrifice and compromise. The failure to successfully negotiate this stage of adult development usually indicates a fear of losing one's own identity. This fear causes the avoidance of intimacy and results in self-absorption and a deep sense of isolation. In extreme cases, says Erikson, this isolation can lead a person to view others as competitors or enemies, to be fought and defeated. More commonly, the failure to enter into deep, meaningful relationships leaves a person affectively immature and fearful of others. A life without intimacy is not only lonely, but is also superficial and unfulfilling.

Close human relationships are integral to experiencing the fullness of life that God invites us to enjoy, and for this reason are vitally important in a holistic spirituality. Contrary to dualistic spiritualities which pit intimacy with God against human intimacy, a holistic spirituality believes that we are not required to choose between loving God and loving others. Human intimacy needs must not be denied in favor of God's love. God did not intend that we live without human affection and love. And we cannot escape the challenges of mature adulthood by spiritualizing our intimacy needs in the false hope that God will directly fulfill them for us. The idea that a person can bypass the human condition and be made whole and holy by the intervention of God is wishful thinking by those who unconsciously seek to avoid the involvements and difficulties of adult life. There is nothing in the life and teaching of Jesus to support such a spirituality. In fact, the gospels clearly show us that to be Christian is to have a love life with each other, as well as with the Wholly Other. Intimacy, our longing for it and our fear of it, can become the crucible in which our wholeness is forged.

Jesus came to manifest God's love and to invite us to participate in that love. Our ability to do so depends on our becoming reconciled to ourselves, to others, and to all creation. The three loves—love of self, others, and God—are intimately connected. A profound experience of any one of these loves nurtures and sustains the others. For example, being deeply touched by God's grace in prayer helps us more fully love ourselves and others; loving and being loved by others help us to better love ourselves and God. Psychologists believe that we must know ourselves as loved before we can love ourselves and others. When Jesus healed people, it was to give them a personal experience of God's compassionate love. Compassion allows us to embrace ourselves with new acceptance. It enables us to love ourselves as we are and moves us to go beyond ourselves to be for others. It is not surprising, then, that the Gerasene demoniac cured by Jesus immediately asked to become a disciple and to join in Jesus' work (Mk 5:18-19). His newly found self-love impelled him into service. Thus, any attempt on our part to grow in self-love and self-acceptance is not a digression from the Christian vocation to love, but rather where any effort to love must begin.

SEXUALITY AND INTIMACY

Our efforts to grow in self-love must include our sexuality, our embodied self. A spirituality that neglects the body, as if it were of no importance in our love life with God and others, fosters in us a dualistic split that undermines our spiritual growth. Equally damaging are attitudes that set the body and spirit at odds, instilling the belief that sensuality and sexuality are anti-Christian and even sinful. A holistic Christian spirituality, on the other hand, regards sexuality as intrinsically connected to our capacity to love because it is as body-persons, as sexual beings, that we relate to others. Many of us, brought up to fear our sexuality as "dirty" or "sinful," treat our sexual life as if it should not be part of us. Often our sexuality resides in the shadow, rejected and outcast, leaving our hearts cold and making generous and joyful self-giving impossible.

The whole area of sexuality is so clouded by anxiety, prejudice, guilt, and sheer ignorance that we must continually remind ourselves of what the incarnation means—that God took on flesh in order to be one with us. Christ, the Word made flesh, made his home in the same human body that is our home. When we deny the goodness of our bodies, we reject the God who chose to have a body. Although the sexuality of Jesus is not explicitly mentioned in the gospels, we must not interpret this to mean that he was not as human as we are or that he was asexual, more spirit than body. On the contrary, the gospel portrait of Jesus is of a man whose sexuality radiated out to others, involving him intimately in their lives. People were drawn to him and he to them. Often moved by compassion, he spontaneously reached out to touch (Mk 1:42), to feed (Mk 6:30-34), and to hold (Mk 10:16), exhibiting a love so passionate that it demanded bodily expression beyond mere words. As followers of Jesus, sexuality is of central importance in our journey toward wholeness and holiness. Only when we are at home in our body, gracefully accepting ourselves as sexual beings, will we be able to securely and freely enter into loving relationships and commitments.

SELF-INTIMACY

The longing for intimacy seems to be at the very core of our being and motivates much of human behavior. Its opposite, power, is the shadow side of intimacy. When we unconsciously fear the vulnerability of intimacy, the desire for it will be repressed and replaced by the desire for power. The ability to relate intimately with others is a sign of psychological development and is not possible until we have achieved a certain degree of personal identity and maturity. The Jewish philosopher Martin Buber introduced the term "I–Thou" relationship to describe the nature of intimacy, in which two distinct persons, each with his or her own identity, choose to cross over into the world of the other. His term connotes respect, separateness, and consciousness. An "I–Thou" relationship with another requires that we first have an intimate relationship with ourselves. Until the shadow has been recognized and to some extent assimilated, we do not have an I–Thou relationship with ourselves and so cannot begin to form I–Thou relationships with others. Intimate relationships depend on an inner connection: to be in touch with another, I must be in touch with myself. On the other hand, it is primarily through relationships that we learn about ourselves. Reflecting on our reactions and responses to others is a road to consciousness. The difficulties we experience in our relationships can be a rich, though painful, path to self-knowledge. Nothing is born into consciousness without suffering. This is why intimacy is only possible with psychological maturity and a willingness to suffer for the sake of growth.

THE NEED FOR A RELIGIOUS ATTITUDE

Psychological growth and transformation require what Jung called a "religious attitude," which means an attitude of reflection and reverent consideration of the conflicts and sufferings which life gives us. The religious attitude does not run from pain or blame others for it, but rather accepts, in the manner of Christ, that suffering can be meaningful and instructive. This is not meant to justify an irresponsible passivity or a pseudo-religiosity that counsels victims of violence and abuse to accept their pain as God's will. The point is that suffering is a universal reality and we must find a way to deal with it. If we humbly and carefully reflect on our painful experiences, we open ourselves to the growth and transformation that can come through suffering. This tenet of depth psychology corresponds with the Christian notion of the "dark night," times of suffering when we are challenged to believe that our painful experiences are not for naught, but actually moments of obscure, yet transforming grace, when God is deepening our capacity for intimate union. When Paul speaks of "putting on the mind of Christ," he is referring to the humility of Jesus, "who, though he was God, learned through suffering" (Heb 5:8).

There is an axiom in Jungian psychology that says, "Work on yourself and good relationships will follow." The truth is that most people begin to discover their need to "work on" themselves only after things have gone badly in their relationships. It is not uncommon that the search for deeper self-knowledge is initiated by love's sufferings: the break-up of a marriage, the failure to find a suitable mate, lack of sexual desire, chronic conflict with a spouse or colleagues, betrayal in friendship, estrangement from a son or daughter, feelings of isolation and loneliness. These typical human problems become the pathway to greater consciousness and understanding.

FROM UNCONSCIOUS TO CONSCIOUS RELATIONSHIP

We often underestimate the complexity of human relationships and the inner and outer reactions that are activated by our contact with others. We dream of the perfect relationship: one that will bring us love and happiness and make us whole; one in which we will be completely understood and fulfilled, and in which we will never again feel pain or fear. Not included in this image, of course, are things like conflict, suffering, sacrifice, or even the awareness that imperfect human beings will have imperfect relationships. Often it is with such unrealistic fantasies that we enter into relationships. When our fantasies come up against reality, which will happen as soon as the relationship moves toward intimacy, we experience a rude awakening. We cannot rub up against people for very long without discovering that we and they are more complex than we thought, and that the ideal of togetherness and harmony, which is based on the archetypal motif of wholeness, paradoxically involves separation and conflict. The idea that all we have to do is find our soul-mate and we will live happily ever after is the stuff of romance novels, but not of real life. The ideal of togetherness is blind to individual differences and the natural boundaries that exist between people. Although, as Jung says, we cannot individuate without relationships, individuation is not about the union of two individualities into one. That is called symbiosis. While many intimate relationships begin in a symbiotic state, sooner or later this psychologically inviable fusion will break down. Conflicts and disagreements introduce reality into what was an "unreal" harmony. As unconscious identifications are broken, both persons are led to an awareness and acceptance of the inner truth of their own natures. And the union and wholeness they each projected onto the relationship must now be found within themselves. As difficult and painful as this "breaking up" process is, it is the sacrifice of our unconscious projections that paves the way for the realization of conscious love and intimacy between two people.

ANIMA/ANIMUS PROJECTIONS

Relationships with persons of the same sex tend to be easier to develop than those with the opposite sex, because with someone of our own sex we have a sense of knowing or of being able to feel into the other. Men, for example, understand what makes other men tick, but are often puzzled by the reactions of women. With the opposite sex, we encounter strangeness or unlikeness. It is this very difference between the sexes that creates a magnetic attraction, the pull of opposites toward each other. When this pull is strong and compelling, yet unexplainable, an unconscious archetypal image has been stimulated. In the case of a woman, it is the image of the masculine; for a man, it is the image of the feminine. Jung explains that "every man carries within him the eternal image of woman, not the image of this or that particular woman, but a definite feminine image."[4] The same is true for women who have an inborn image of man. This contrasexual image, which in men is called the "anima" and in women is called the "animus," is an archetype, a psychic imprint. As with all unconscious images, we meet them first in projected form, in this case, in a person of the opposite sex. A major difference between shadow projections and animus/anima projections is that the shadow represents the part of our personal unconscious which has been rejected, whereas the contrasexual image is an autonomous archetype, whose source is the collective or non-personal unconscious. Because they are aspects of our own personality which we dislike, shadow projections are negatively toned. In contrast, anima/animus projections tend to fascinate us and exert an unexplainable hold over us. This is what happens when we fall in love. Each person who fascinates us is stimulating something in our own psyche which wants to come to life.

Heterosexual relationships are usually sparked off by animus/anima projections. When we first fall in love with someone, for example, we are more infatuated with our projected image of the other than with the real flesh-and-blood person. A genuine relationship, however, cannot develop as long as our projections remain intact. To the degree that a relationship is based on projection, it is lacking in genuine human love. "To be in love with someone we do not know as a person, but are attracted to because they reflect back to us the image of the god or goddess in our souls," states John Sanford, "is, in a sense, to be in love with oneself, not with the other person."[5] Authentic love begins when we get to know others as they really are as human beings and come to care for them.

Projections distort the reality of the other person, who may in fact be quite different than our image of them. Until we recognize and withdraw our projections, we will suffer the effects of pseudo-relationships in the form of disappointed expectations and feelings of being "let down" by the other person when he or she does not behave according to our image. The more unrealistic our expectations, the more frequent these disillusioning experiences will be, until we are forced to withdraw our projections and see the other as he or she truly is. This is no easy task and often involves great effort and suffering. Not only do we have to face our illusions about the other person, but we must also find within ourselves what we have been looking for in the other. Until we confront our anima or animus and develop a living, growing relationship with it, we will continue to project our inner other onto the opposite sex.

INTEGRATING BOTH ANIMA AND ANIMUS

The animus represents the human potential for action and relates us to our ability for rational thought as well as our capacity for self-assertion and taking a stand. The anima, on the other hand, represents the human potential for receptivity and opens us to the world of emotions and relationships. Usually, a woman's individuation requires integrating the animus, and a man's, the anima. But there are men who for reasons of upbringing or culture have a better relationship to their anima than to their animus and women who have a better relationship to their animus than to their anima. In any case, individuation requires that we work to integrate whatever human potentials have been neglected.

Whether we are male or female, we all possess the same human attributes and drives, and these potentials want to be expressed.

When we are not consciously related to them, our personalities suffer because our development is stunted. For example, a woman who does not develop at least some of her potential for assertion and independent thinking (animus) will remain caught in the stereotype of the sweet, loving, motherly woman whose thoughts mirror what she hears from "authorities." In other words, she will not know what she herself thinks and feels; nor will she be capable of saying "no" to anyone or anything, because she will not have the personal boundaries that come with self-knowledge. And in turn a man's failure to at least minimally integrate his anima will result in a personality that is all head and no heart. He may achieve success because of his ambition, intellect, and aggressiveness, but his emotional development and capacity for relationships will be stymied.

A good relationship with the anima and animus brings a feeling of wholeness, and frees us from depending on someone of the opposite sex to complete us. Many conflicts and frustrations in relationships between the sexes arise because of unconscious expectations that the other must supply what we are lacking. This can be seen in women who expect men to be a "rock of Gibraltar," a hero who rescues them from distress; or in men who count on women to be an "earth mother," available whenever they need her to fulfill their physical and emotional needs. Intimate relationships are less stressful and more fulfilling when, for example, women develop their own strength and independence, instead of relying on men for these qualities, and when men develop their own emotional awareness and responsiveness, instead of relying on the women in their lives to do this for them. Such psychological development frees a relationship from the burden of unconscious projections and makes possible a relationship of equality and mutuality.

DEVELOPING A RELATIONSHIP WITH THE INNER "THOU"

Developing a relationship to our anima or animus deepens our self-knowledge and capacity for real relatedness and intimacy. How this relationship develops is not unlike the way a relationship with our shadow develops. We learn about the contrasexual image we carry within in much the same way we learn about our shadow. Dreams are an excellent source of information. Here a man's anima appears in feminine figures and symbols, and a woman's animus will reach out to her in male figures and symbols. In our waking life, we can examine the qualities of the men, if we are a woman, and of the women, if we are a man, who fascinate and attract us. Television programs, movies, plays, and literature also attract our projections, as we fall in love with one character and come to hate another.

Society's stereotypes of masculine and feminine also inform us about our anima and animus. In a culture that rigidly differentiates sex roles, people are likely to internalize and identify with whatever the dominant culture defines as typically "male" and typically "female," and repress those characteristics that do not fit. Recognizing and challenging these sexual stereotypes is an important step in reclaiming our wholeness.

Active imagination, a method of dialogue with inner figures and images, is another helpful tool in getting to know the anima and animus. Dialoguing with the male and female images in our dreams and fantasies reveals just what we expect from, or feel about, men and women. Actively imagining these contrasexual figures and conversing with them help us recognize and claim those capabilities which we project onto the opposite sex.[6]

As our consciousness develops, we come to realize that there is both masculine and feminine, lover and beloved within us, and that the sense of fulfillment we depended on another person to give us is available to us when we relate deeply with our own soul. Anima and animus images inform us of our human ideals, of what life means to us, and what is possible for us. The process of recognizing and integrating our projections establishes a bridge to the unconscious "other" within, making possible a loving and life-giving union of the masculine and feminine energies inside ourselves. From this marriage of the opposites is born a sense of individuality and personal integrity that frees us to relate to others in their individuality. We know ourselves as separate from, yet equal to, others and are able to respect the natural boundaries between people. This is the basis of intimacy.

AFFAIRS OF THE HEART: THE VALUE OF FALLING IN LOVE

When we "work on" ourselves, we improve our capacity to relate to other people; when we "work on" our relationships and the unconscious elements that influence them, we accelerate our personal development. The "stuff of life" happens between people. And when a human relationship is important to us, when our emotions and libido are invested in it, that relationship can become a vehicle for our psychological growth and individuation. Individuation, the process of growing into our unique selves, cannot take place in a vacuum. Affairs of the heart, even when they are one-sided, set in motion a psychological process of inner development. Being in such a relationship stretches us, challenging our comfortable defenses and habits. The give-and-take of intimate interactions requires that we be honest about our feelings, needs, and desires, work through inevitable conflicts and misunderstandings, and be open to previously unknown aspects of ourselves. As one psychologist put it, "Intimate relationships always ask us to give up something we cherish: certain favorite privacies, preferences, or ways of staying securely defended. They require us to take a leap beyond our usual style of defending our personal territory."[7] Only another human being can make us conscious of the many sides of ourselves of which we are unaware. Because human relationships involve real values, desires, and emotions, they are capable of bringing about great psychological and spiritual transformation.

Besides being transforming, love relationships are also affirming. To be in love is one of life's most wondrous experiences. When we are in love everything takes on new meaning. Life is no longer ordinary and mundane, but is suddenly exciting and filled with rich possibilities. Being the object of someone's love and devotion deeply transforms our sense of self and gives us a glimpse of who we are in the eyes of the one who created us. The best in us comes out and is, in fact, drawn out by the love of the beloved who sees our potential and encourages it. In this lies the hidden power of love, that we are given the vision to see something in the other which that person may have sensed but perhaps may never have known had it not been for our loving affirmation.

In the early stage of love we project onto the one we love, not only what we lack, but also what we intuitively see in that person. The beloved is more than a mirror in which we can discover ourselves; through the vision love gives us, we imaginatively see the best in the beloved and project that too, giving that person the feeling that those potentials can be achieved. This is why people in love see things in each other that those who do not love them cannot see.

The familiar saying, "Love is blind," is not completely true, because love also gives us a kind of intuitive insight into the depths of the beloved. And as Jungian writer Verena Kast expresses it, "In such a state of love, we dare all, we feel that we can give all, and these feelings enliven the fantasies of relationship and intensify love."[8] The idealization that goes on in new love enhances our self-esteem and graces us with a sense of self-worth and well-being that moves us to grow beyond ourselves.

RELATIONSHIP AS A CONTAINER FOR GROWTH

When we speak of a containing relationship we mean one which has the capacity to hold or include all of who we are. In such a relationship, we are free to be ourselves without the fear of rejection or punishment that characterizes codependent relationships. A containing relationship promotes our growth in consciousness and wholeness because it makes space for the shadow to emerge. Many of us, because we grew up in dysfunctional families, think that to be in relationship, we must submerge parts of ourselves and settle for being less than who we are. Although we may long for relationships in which we can be ourselves, having been deprived of this experience in childhood, we tend to doubt the possibility of finding it in adulthood. If we learned that love and acceptance were conditional on pleasing others, it may take a big leap of faith to trust that there can be a kind of love that embraces all of who we are. When we find this level of acceptance, we are able to overcome our own self-rejection.

Developing a containing relationship with another person or within a group requires that we make a commitment to our own personal growth and value that same personal growth in others. This does not mean that we are free of complexes, childhood wounds and unconscious projections, for this is an impossibility. But it does mean that we have some consciousness of those issues and how they affect our emotional responses to ourselves and to others. Unresolved issues from our childhood will repeatedly get acted out as relationship issues in the present. For example, early experiences of abandonment may be reawakened in a close friendship, causing us to see our friend as the source of our fear of loss. As long as our abandonment fears are projected onto our friend, we will react in exaggerated ways, for instance, clinging to this person out of fear of losing him or her. This clinging behavior, while manifesting itself in the present, has its roots in the past. Consciousness of this abandonment issue will help us to better understand and resolve some of the conflicts that arise in our relationships.

COMMITMENT IN CONTAINING RELATIONSHIPS

Containing relationships, whether in marriage, Christian community, or friendship, involve a threefold commitment to "love, honor, and obey," to use the familiar words from the traditional marriage vow. "To love" means to love as God loves, inclusively and without demands. "To honor" means that we respect the freedom and integrity of the other and do not judge what we do not understand. "To obey" means listening and responding with sincerity and honesty to the truth of the other person. This threefold commitment must also be made interiorly with oneself. For if we do not relate to ourselves in a manner that is loving, obedient, and respectful of our own unique being, we cannot develop such a relationship with others.

If a relationship is to serve as a container for growth, it must be able to endure the seasons that all relationships inevitably go through. A relationship that flourishes when all is well, but flounders when difficulties arise, is a fair-weather relationship, not a containing relationship. Jungian analyst Adolf Guggenbühl-Craig distinguishes between two very different attitudes toward intimate relationships.[9] The first, which is the most popular, is that relationships, whether in marriage, friendship or community life, should be pleasurable and make us feel good. This view, which sees the goal of relationship as well-being, values comfort, ease, and happiness above all else. It strives to avoid the pain and discomfort that commonly arise in human relationships and flees from commitment when the going gets tough. People who are motivated solely by this attitude often go from relationship to relationship in search of others who will not challenge them with "petty" and "unimportant" relationship issues and feelings, but instead will gratify their egocentric needs.

The second attitude toward intimacy is that relationships are a vehicle for consciousness and individuation. In this view, relationships serve a spiritual purpose, that of working out our salvation in the "for better or worse" of commitments. This basically Christian notion suggests that the creative and salvific work of marriage or of any other committed relationship is in the acceptance of the joy and sorrow, pain and pleasure, conflict and harmony which are the polarities of life.

Sacrifice for the Sake of Wholeness

Intimate relationships are not meant to be exclusively comfortable and harmonious; rather they are containers for individuation in which persons rub up against each other and so learn to know themselves, the world, good and evil, the heights and the depths. Holistic Christian spirituality views metanoia and sacrifice as indispensable for achieving wholeness and salvation. To become the person God created us to be, we must, paradoxically, be willing to renounce or sacrifice some parts of ourselves, as the biblical story of Abraham and Isaac dramatically portrays. Sacrifice in this sense differs from martyrdom in that it is freely chosen for the sake of wholeness. For example, in the close cheek by jowl living that married life entails, spouses inevitably bump up against each other's areas of unconsciousness and hurt each other without intending to. When the hurtful quality or trait is objected to by one partner, the other is challenged to examine the feedback honestly. This affords married couples a chance to become aware of shadow qualities or habits that they recognize only when their companions in daily life complain about them. If the spouses value the relationship over their own self-image and are committed to love, honor, and obey, they will stay open to their partner's objection and own up to any aspect of their shadow that has caused hurt. Egotistic attachment to self-image is counterproductive in relationships where people want to grow in intimacy. Admitting how we have unconsciously hurt someone we love requires a sacrifice of our ego and a willingness to change by becoming conscious. If we value intimate relationships only when they provide us with a sense of happiness and well-being, our relationships will always be on shaky ground. But if we value our relationships as a crucible for holiness and wholeness, we will have the perseverance and commitment to "stay with" and "work

through" the difficulties that arise. In this way, intimate relationships can expand both our self-knowledge and our capacity to love.

A story in novelist Andrew Greeley's *The Cardinal Virtues*
delightfully highlights how marriage can be a durable container for
growth and how God, the Earth Maker, is also intimately involved in
the struggles that are part and parcel of all committed relationships.
In the novel, a minister, while officiating at a wedding, tells a story
about why Earth Maker made strawberries.[10] "Once upon a time,
long, long ago," he began with a county Kerry brogue, "First Man
and First Woman were living happily together" and Earth Maker, a
good friend, often visited them in their little cottage on the edge of
the bogs. They had their occasional arguments, but nothing ever
serious. Then one day, "a real rip-roaring donnybrook" flared up
and angry words flew between them about who started the fight
and then about what the first fight had been about. Finally, First
Woman stormed out, yelling "You're nothing but a flannel mouth
idjit" and "I'm sick of you." Fueled by her anger, she speedily
crossed the field, dashed down into the valley and over the hill
beyond, never once looking back. Initially, First Man breathed a
sigh of relief, thinking how he'd finally enjoy some peace and quiet.
But as the sun set over the ocean, First Man's relief gave way to
sadness as he stared at the barren house. Even as his stomach
growled, he realized he was too sick with loneliness to eat. So, he
tried to escape his loneliness through sleep. But the bed was terribly
cold and his sleep was fitful. When morning finally came, First Man
was surprised by a visit from Earth Maker, who quickly inquired
about herself. "Ah, she's gone, your Reverence; stormed out on me,"
replied First Man defensively. When asked why, he stammered and
finally admitted, "To tell you the truth, your Reverence, I can't
remember." Seeing how heartbroken First Man looked, Earth Maker
said to him, "Well then, man, on your way. Go chase her and ask her
to come back." First Man jumped at the idea, but was soon
discouraged about being able to catch up to First Woman who had
such a big head start. But at Earth Maker's encouragement, he
rushed out the door, crossed the field and dashed down the valley
and over the hill beyond.

Moving ahead of him, Earth Maker spotted First Woman still
striding along at a rapid clip and realized that he'd have to work
some wonders to slow her down so that First Man could catch up.
With divine panache, Earth Maker put a great forest smack in the

way of First Woman. But to no avail, since she zoomed through it like a knife through hot butter. Earth Maker, thinking that First Woman would be mighty hungry by now, quickly sprung a fruit orchard in her path. But First Woman wasted no time to stop to eat. Instead, she picked the fruit on the fly and ate on the run.

Finally, Earth Maker smiled and realized that she had to rely on her ultimate contingency in order to retard the fierce speed of First Woman. So *zap*, up shot a strawberry bush with beautiful white flowers and lovely red strawberries. First Woman was fascinated that the berries had the same shape and color as the human heart. Touching a berry, she thought it resembled the human heart, soft and yet firm. Then she tasted one. "Och," First Woman said, "isn't it the sweetest taste in all the world. Sure, the only thing sweeter is human love." And as she's eating the berry and thinking of human love, her mind drifted to First Man. "Ah, the poor man," she thought. "He's after trying to catch up with me and by the time he does, won't he be perishing with the hunger. I know what I'll do. I'll just pick some more of these strawberries, and we'll eat them when he catches up. Then we'll go home together." First Man finally met up with First Woman and together they ate the strawberries. Then hand in hand they returned home, with Earth Maker smiling along behind them.

As a final word to the newlyweds, the story-telling minister said: "Now I'm warning you...from now on whenever you eat strawberries...remember my story and know again that the only thing sweeter than the taste of strawberries is human love. And...ask yourself is there someone waiting now for me to catch up. Or should I wait for someone who is trying to catch up with me?"

A containing relationship, one in which we are committed to waiting for each other, is both a gift and a creative work. We cannot make such a relationship happen. We can, however, be open to it, looking for opportunities to create conscious relationships with others and welcoming those that invite us to grow beyond ourselves. Containing relationships are not necessarily romantic relationships, although marriage is the relationship in which this happens for many people. Friendships, therapeutic relationships, and intentional communities, when those involved are equally committed to their own and each other's growth, also have the potential for becoming containers for growth.

HUMAN INTIMACY AS A SCHOOL OF LOVE

We are meant to enjoy intimacy with God here on earth as well as in the hereafter. As spiritual writer Evelyn Underhill put it so beautifully, "God is one who stoops towards us and first incites and then supports and responds to our seeking."[11] In our earthly lives, the intimacy that we share with loved ones is very often the experience that best reveals the face of God to us. To the apostle Philip's request to "see the Father," Jesus responded, "To have seen me is to have seen the Father, so how can you say, 'Let us see the Father?'" (Jn 14:9-10). Enigmatic as it may sound, Jesus' response comes down to this: he can show us what God is only by the way he reflects God in his own humanity. He can reveal the face of God only by showing us his own face.[12] Theologian Monika Hellwig summarizes the truth of how God is revealed in our intimate knowledge of a friend: "As Christians, we see Jesus as the unique image of God in humanity. But we also see Jesus as prototypical and inclusive of us all, drawing us into his witness and his ministry of reconciliation and reconstruction, making us in union with him a kind of temple where God is to be encountered, experienced, and brought to others."[13] Therefore, intimate friendships, which embody the love of Christ, can be for us a kind of temple where we can see the face of God.

Hellwig's insight is beautifully illustrated by a story about how two brothers' love for each other transformed their intimate relationship into a temple, where God was made known.

> Time before time, when the world was young, two brothers shared a field and a mill, each night dividing evenly the grain they had ground together during the day. One brother lived alone; the other had a wife and a large family. Now the single brother thought to himself one day, "It isn't really fair that we divide the grain evenly. I have only myself to care for, but my brother has children to feed." So each night he secretly took some of his grain to his brother's granary to see that he was never without.
>
> But the married brother said to himself one day, "It isn't really fair that we divide the grain evenly, because I have children to provide for me in my old age, but my brother has no one. What will he do when he's old?" So every night he secretly took some of *his* grain to his brother's granary. As a result, both of them always found their supply of grain mysteriously replenished each morning.

Then one night they met each other halfway between their two houses, suddenly realized what had been happening, and embraced each other in love. The story is that God witnessed their meeting and proclaimed, "This is a holy place—a place of love—and here it is that my temple shall be built." And so it was. The holy place, where God is made known to...people, is the place where human beings discover each other in love.[14]

Intimacy is a locus of divine revelation because, as this story points out, God who is Incarnate Love is encountered in the fleshy experience of human love. Human intimacy is also a school of love that prepares our hearts for eternal intimacy with God. Intimate relationships, with all their joys and sorrows, are truly a crucible for wholeness when they deepen our capacity to love with integrity and faithfulness and allow us to love as Jesus did.

Reflection Questions

1. Discuss the relationship between intimacy and Christian living. What is the relationship between sexuality and spirituality?

2. What in your personality makeup and past experience helps you form and enjoy intimate relationships? What makes intimacy difficult and problematic for you?

3. Discuss how projections (both shadow and anima/animus) cause problems in intimate relationships. How would a containing relationship deal constructively with projections?

CHAPTER EIGHT

COMPASSION AND COLLABORATION: LOVING WITH THE WHOLE SELF

We witness to God's compassionate presence in the world by the way we live
and work together.... Compassion always reveals itself in community, in a new
way of being together.[1]
—Donald McNeill
Douglas Morrison
Henri Nouwen
COMPASSION

TEARS OF SHAME and guilt were already streaming down his face, as
he dashed out of the courtyard of the high priest's house where
Jesus was being detained. "How could you have so blatantly betrayed
your friend Jesus?" asked a harsh inner voice. Just a while ago, the
thought of turning his back on Jesus was simply unthinkable. His
words to Jesus, recently spoken with such bravado, now came back
to haunt him: "I would be ready to go to prison with you, and to
death" (Lk 22:34).

But just as Jesus had predicted, he had ended up denying the
Lord three times tonight. It had all happened so fast, thought Peter.
First, he found himself following cautiously, all the way into the
courtyard. Then, as he started getting self-conscious about being
recognized as a follower of Jesus, it dawned on him that he himself
was in danger. That's when the people started accusing him out
loud: "You too were with Jesus, the man from Nazareth" (Mk 15:68).
He could feel himself tense up. The more people pressed the issue,

the more adamant became his denial. In a matter of minutes, his shrug of denial grew into a full-blown oath, when he started calling down curses on himself and swearing, "I do not know the man" (Mt 26:74). Even as he recalled the swift sequence of events, the bitter pain of failure knotted his stomach and he felt weighed down by depression. Peter later realized that the look of Jesus in the courtyard when the Lord turned toward him—a look so full of compassion—is what jarred him into the awareness that he had done a terrible thing *and* that Jesus understood and forgave him. When that realization hit him, he dissolved into tears.

That all four gospels recount Peter's denial indicates that the early church proclaimed, not covered up, their first leader's deficiency. Somehow, they were strengthened, not scandalized, by it. Peter's experience reaffirmed for them that it is okay to fail, because forgiveness is always available. Very likely, Peter himself had spread the story of his failure, as he tirelessly tried to strengthen the brothers and sisters in their struggles—as Jesus had asked him to do. "Simon, Simon! Satan, you must know, has got his wish to sift you all like wheat; but I have prayed for you, Simon, that your faith may not fail, and once you have recovered, you in turn must strengthen others" (Lk 22:31-33). Just as the early Christians saw Adam's fall as a "happy fault," because it brought forth a Savior, they also regarded Peter's slip as a "*felix culpa*," for it gave them a compassionate leader. Peter had been forced to face his shadow and had been made humble and compassionate as a result.

SHADOW-WORK AND COMPASSION

Peter's experience points out a universal truth: the more we face our shadow, the more compassionate we become. As mentioned in Chapter Two, St. Teresa encouraged the ongoing pursuit of self-knowledge, because it leads to humility, the graceful awareness and acceptance of our fragility and limitations as creatures. Humility draws us to God with poverty of spirit and to others with compassion. True self-knowledge lays bare the fact that each of us is part light and part darkness, part angel and part monster. Whenever we identify solely with the light, angelic side of our being, we separate ourselves from others in a spirit of self-righteousness and pride. When, however, we recognize the dark, monstrous potential that is also ours—as in St. Augustine's confession, "There but for the grace of God go I!"—we draw closer to others in solidarity and compassion. If we find that we are easily scandalized or hear ourselves repeatedly saying, "How could anyone ever do such a horrible thing?" we may need to plumb the depths once again to meet our shadow.

SHADOW-WORK AND CHRISTIAN GROWTH

The kind of shadow-work described in this book is central to spiritual development because compassionate love is the core of Christian discipleship. To imitate Jesus is to love with compassion. The plight of individuals and groups always stirred Jesus' heart and moved him to reach out in healing, forgiving, and nourishing ways. For example, once a leper approached Jesus, begging to be cured (Mk 1:40-45). Jesus took in the reality of this afflicted suppliant, paying close attention to his words and actions. Then, moved with compassion, he reached out to touch the diseased person. Jesus' therapeutic touch issued forth from a compassionate heart. His response to this leper, ostracized from society on account of his ailment, was typical of Jesus. Other outcasts of his day—women, foreigners, tax collectors, and prostitutes—also received compassion from Jesus, even as their religious leaders denied them access to the official channels of healing and reconciliation.

The needs of groups also called forth the compassionate concern of Jesus. In Mark's two accounts of the multiplication of the loaves and the fishes (6:30-44; 8:1-10), it was Jesus' compassion for the crowd that moved him to act. As he cast his eyes upon the hungry throng which had gathered to feed on his words, he said to his disciples, "I feel sorry for all these people; they have been with me for three days now and have nothing to eat. If I send them off home hungry they will collapse on the way; some have come from a great distance" (8:2-4). The first Markan account of the miracle of the loaves states that Jesus ordered the disciples "to get the people together in groups on the green grass, and they sat down on the ground in squares of hundreds and fifties" (Mk 6:39-41). According to scripture scholar Edward J. Mally, this statement "is possibly an allusion to Moses' apportioning the Israelites into groups...(Ex 18:25; Dt 1:15),"[2] and to the feeding of the Israelites with manna in the desert. The compassion of Jesus in feeding the multitude resembles the compassion of Yahweh who fed the liberated Israelites with manna from heaven as they made their painful escape from Egypt through the wilderness. This resemblance is not surprising since the mission of Jesus was to embody the compassion of God.

JESUS, THE COMPASSION OF GOD

Compassion characterized the person of Jesus as well as his mission. Ignatius of Loyola, in guiding a person's contemplation of the incarnation, paints a vivid picture of the mission of Jesus.[3] He asks the person making the Spiritual Exercises to imagine how the Trinity hovers over the globe, perceiving the wounds of the world with sensitivity and care. At the sight of people of all colors, creeds, ages, and backgrounds struggling and lost, like sheep without a shepherd, the persons of the Trinity are moved with compassion. They then decide that one of them should become human to enable people to experience concretely God's empathic concern. So the Word becomes flesh or, as John's gospel puts it, "pitched his tent among us" (1:14). This Ignatian contemplation invites us to appreciate how God was not satisfied to love us from afar, but drew near in the person of Jesus. Throughout his life, and especially during his public ministry, Jesus accomplished his mission of incarnating the compassion of God for suffering humanity by proclaiming the good news to the poor, giving sight to the blind, healing the broken-hearted, comforting the afflicted, and setting captives free. Before departing, he commissioned his disciples and the community he founded to continue his mission. Baptism hands that commission on to us, the Christian community. Ministry, broadly understood, refers to the wide variety of ways that Christians in all walks of life continue Christ's compassionate presence in the world today.

DISCIPLESHIP: A CALL TO EMBODY THE COMPASSION OF JESUS

Whatever form our lives take, we are called as Christians to minister, to give flesh-and-blood reality to the ongoing compassion of God for all. Today God depends on us to embody the love of Jesus for others, as the following story emphasizes: A statue of Jesus wrecked by the shelling during the war stood just outside a small village near Normandy. Its hands had been totally destroyed. After the war, the villagers gathered around the ruined statue to decide its fate. One group argued that the statue was so badly damaged that it should be trashed and a new one erected in its place. Another group objected, arguing that the village artisan whose specialty was the restoration of damaged art objects could easily take care of the job. Finally, a third group voiced a proposal that ultimately carried the day: that the statue be cleaned up, but remain handless; and that a plaque be placed at its base with the inscription: "I have no hands but yours."

Similarly, the story of a young man killed in a drive-by shooting illustrates how ministry calls us to stand in place of Jesus for those who cry out for love and reassurance. The wounded man lay dying in front of the church, as a group of horrified parishioners gathered around him, waiting for the paramedics to arrive. As his life energies steadily slipped away, the young man could be heard over and over again crying out for his mother, seemingly to no avail. Suddenly, a woman broke through the crowd and bent down to cradle the dying man in her arms. Gently rocking him, she repeated in assuring tones, "I'm here, son. Everything's going to be okay." As the dying man breathed his last breath, she blessed him with the sign of the cross.

A few days later, the woman, filled with scruples, appeared at the door of the rectory. She wanted to confess that she had lied, that she was not really the mother of the young man who had died. She felt guilty for what she had done, even though at the time she felt drawn to do whatever was needed to comfort the dying man crying out for his mother. She left the rectory with peace of mind and a sense of validation, because the priest had reassured her that she not only had done nothing wrong, but, in fact, responded in a most Christlike way. Like Jesus, she had embodied the compassion of God for another.

COMMUNITY MAKES COMPASSION POSSIBLE

Left to ourselves as individuals, there is no way we can continue the compassionate response of Christ for the wounds of humanity. Only together in community can we hope to do so. Alone, we feel overwhelmed and helpless, even discouraged and depressed, when faced with the magnitude and extent of human suffering. Community is the reality that makes it possible for us to see the enormity of the pain in our world and still be moved to compassion as Jesus was when he saw a large crowd of people without food.

Through the miracle of the multiplication of the loaves, Jesus taught his disciples a valuable lesson: community, where creating and sharing together generates abundance, "is the context in which abundance can replace scarcity."[4] Faced with their limited supply of food, only five loaves and two fish, the disciples' initial response to the problem of the hungry crowd was to "send them away, to go into the country and villages round about" to buy their own food (Mk 6:35-37). Instead, Jesus instructed the disciples to divide the crowd into smaller groups, in which people could shed their anonymity and encounter each other in their mutual need. Direct contact with others caught in the same predicament made a decisive difference, as Parker Palmer points out:

> In the faceless crowd we experience scarcity—a scarcity of contact, of concern, of affirmation, of love. But as the crowd is replaced by community, an invisible sense of abundance arises long before the community produces any visible goods or services. True abundance resides in the simple experience of people being present to one another and for one another. Only in such a context of interpersonal abundance could the material abundance of food aplenty even begin to arise.[5]

Today, constant bombardment by electronic news coverage of hardships and tragedies around the world can so overwhelm us that we feel, like the disciples, that it is too much for us to deal with. We have enough trouble coping with the daily difficulties that arise within our small circle of family and friends. However, with the support of the Christian community, we can witness the pain of the human family without turning away or becoming angered by our impotence, because in community we experience the strength and power that come from pooling our resources.[6] Community allows us to benefit from the diverse gifts and charisms possessed by different members who make up the one body of Christ and enables us to reach out to others with the compassion of Jesus. Without community, we can only experience the suffering of others as a crushing and overwhelming burden.

COMMUNITY AND COLLABORATION

In order for community to function as an effective instrument of God's compassion, collaboration among community members is vitally important. The absence of collaboration seriously weakens the ministerial outreach of the Christian community and cripples its ability to respond to those in need. One day a young boy was straining to move a large rock. Walking by, his father asked him, "Son, are you using all your strength?" "Yes, I am," replied the exasperated boy. "No, you're not," the father continued, "because you haven't asked me for help."[7] The adage, "Many hands make light the work," captures the underlying wisdom of human collaboration. Scripture makes clear that God intends us to work together and to support each other: Yahweh made man and woman so that together they might "be fruitful, multiply, and fill the earth" (Gen 1:28), and Jesus sent the seventy-two disciples on their first mission in pairs so that they could labor with mutual support.

Like an idea whose time has come, the concept of collaboration has wide appeal. Yet, many of us have found—often through painful experience—that implementing it is more complicated than we first thought. Tensions and strains inevitably surface when we encounter major differences in theologies and spiritualities, philosophies and worldviews, personalities and temperaments, personal struggles and needs. These differences generate conflict that must be consciously dealt with if collaboration is to succeed. Shared ministry requires that we trade our individualistic and competitive attitudes for ones which appreciate and encourage the unique gifts each member brings to the work of the group. Without a commitment to honest dialogue and a willingness to grow in understanding the dynamics of cooperation, collaborative ministry will fail. In addition to basic communication and group dynamics skills, we also need to appreciate the faith assumptions that support collaborative ministry. These assumptions, when consciously held by the whole group, create a shared vision and common purpose that will motivate and sustain us in our striving to embody God's compassionate love.

Ministry: We Share in God's Action. Each of us has something to offer to the Christian community's effort to embody the compassion of Jesus for others. This growing awareness has resulted in a movement away from an elitist emphasis on "a few are chosen" to a more inclusive insistence that "many are called." In fact, the truth is that all are called to share in the mission of Jesus as a baptismal right. In his *Spiritual Exercises*, St. Ignatius of Loyola tells us that we live in a God-soaked world. Reality is drenched in divinity. Moreover, God's presence in creation is dynamic, not merely inert.

Ignatius directs those making the Spiritual Exercises "to consider how God *works and labors* for [them] in all creatures upon the face of the earth."[8] God is ever in our midst laboring for us. "In the heavens, the elements, the plants, the fruits, the cattle, etc., God gives being, conserves them, confers life and sensation, etc." This ongoing labor of God in the world constitutes the essence of ministry. Given this understanding of ministry as God's pervasive action in the world, it is clear why Ignatius taught: "Pray as if everything depends on you; work as if everything depends on God."[9] The focus in ministry should be on God, not us. We are ministers solely because God has cut us in on the action. God invites us to give human form to the divine presence and love that abound in every nook and cranny of creation. We are called to be, in the words of Ignatius, "contemplatives even in action," people who have a facility for finding God in all things.

Ministry: We Are Placed Intimately with the Son. Another Ignatian image of ministry that supports collaboration is that of our "being placed" by the Father next to Jesus carrying the cross. Jesus carrying the cross symbolizes the redemptive presence of Christ in the world today. By being placed in intimate juxtaposition next to Jesus carrying the cross, we are given the gift of sharing in Jesus' saving work. This image of ministry stems from Ignatius' personal religious experience at a small chapel called La Storta, about ten miles outside of Rome. When he was making his way to Rome to consult with the pope as to how he and his newly formed group of Jesuits could best serve the universal church, he had a vision. In this vision, he experienced his petition to serve Jesus being granted as he heard the Father say to Jesus weighed down by his cross: "It is my will that You take this man [referring to Ignatius] for Your servant," and Jesus in turn saying to Ignatius, "It is My will that you serve Us."[10] Ignatius' experience of being chosen by God to be God's servant resembles St. Paul's understanding of himself as chosen to be a minister of God (2 Cor 6:3f) and minister of Christ (2 Cor 11:23).

Both the image of ministry as God's present labor on behalf of all creation and the image of being placed next to Jesus carrying the cross highlight the essential nature of ministry: it is first and foremost God's work. Strictly speaking, the term "collaborative ministry" is redundant. All ministry is "collaborative" because all of us are coworkers with God. Before ministers are collaborators with each other, they are first of all, in the words of St. Paul, "collaborators of Christ" (1 Cor 3:9). Because ministry is not ours in the first place, nothing can justify a possessive exclusion of others.

Ministry: We Reap What We Have Not Sown. Embedded in the story of Jesus' engaging dialogue with the Samaritan woman at the well, like a pearl lodged in an oyster, is the biblical insight that all ministry is a gift from God. The evangelist John cleverly crafted the overall structure of the dialogue to make one thing starkly clear: it is the Lord who supplies the labor, while others receive a gratuitous share in reaping the rewards.

A brief literary analysis of the text will help us pry open the shell to uncover this gem of an insight. The drama opens with Jesus and his disciples arriving at the well of Jacob near Sychar. Jesus sits down beside the well because he is weary (*kekopiakos*) from the journey (4:6). Later we will discover why Jesus is the one who is tired. The Greek word for weary contains a root, *kop*, which has two different meanings. Besides meaning "tired," it also denotes "labor." The *kop* root, with its second meaning, reappears in v. 38 to form a semitic inclusion, a literary device (serving like bookends) that provides thematic unity to a passage. Here Jesus tells the apostles how blessed they are because "I sent you to reap that for which you did not labor; others have labored (*kekopiakasin*), and you have entered into their labor (*kopon*). Because they will harvest what they themselves did not sow, the disciples' involvement in apostolic work is a gift that Jesus bestows on them. In this passage, the evangelist depicts Jesus as the one who is tired (*kekopiakos*), because he is the one who does all the work. Although they arrived with Jesus, the disciples immediately leave the scene to go shopping. They are noticeably absent for the whole time that Jesus struggles so hard with the Samaritan woman, finally bringing her to faith through painstaking and patient efforts. Only when all the work is done do the disciples reappear.

When we examine Jesus' encounter with the woman, we see what a challenge she presented to Jesus. When he first meets up with her, she is both without faith and without community. Scripture scholars point to the unusual time of her coming to the well as an indication of her alienation from others in the community. Such a chore was usually done in the morning and evening, not at noon, the hottest point of the day. The woman's timing for coming to the well suggests that she had structured her life-style to avoid encounter with others. Living in an ambiguous and shameful moral situation, she might have feared the reproach of her neighbors and the kind of moral probing that could easily expose and embarrass her. Thus she scheduled her daily routine in a way that avoided interpersonal encounter and confrontation. Yet, in her meeting with Jesus, God shatters the constricting structures that she imposed on her life. Through her personal contact with Jesus, dialogue brought to birth both belief and relationship. Jesus' respectful, patient, and non-judgmental manner broke through the Samaritan woman's resistance to encounter: "What? You are a Jew and you ask me, a Samaritan, for a drink?" (4:9); and her deviousness: "I have no husband" (4:17). Clearly, Jesus converted the woman through persistent efforts of his own. The absent disciples were of no help. So on their return, when they witnessed the woman and townspeople embracing the way of Jesus with enthusiastic faith, Jesus pointed out an obvious truth: others have sown what they will have the benefit of reaping. Sharing in the ministry of Jesus, therefore, is an unearned gift that we receive from God, something that we neither deserve nor merit.

If ministry is principally God's work, important questions need to be asked by Christians who together form a community of ministers. What is God about in the world these days, and how can we cooperate with God's hopes and plans? How do we as Christians join together to advance the purposes of God and abet the movements of grace at work in the world today? By prayerfully considering such questions and honestly sharing our insights with one another, we can create a sense of shared vision and common purpose that unifies our efforts and sustains us in working through whatever might divide us.

ACHIEVING A BALANCED LIFE

Working collaboratively in community does not exempt us from taking responsibility for fostering our own ongoing spiritual, emotional, and psychosexual growth and establishing a balanced, holistic spirituality. In fact, collaboration makes more imperative the need to deal honestly with issues related to our own developmental growth. Because personal growth issues directly affect our ability to work effectively with others, we will benefit greatly in our communal endeavors by reflecting on such questions as:

What in me helps or hinders working collaboratively with others?

Am I secure enough to contribute as an equal—respectful of what both I and others have to offer to a common venture? Is my self-esteem solid enough to allow me to affirm others and be content in playing my part or do I have to be in charge all the time?

Is my self-worth so wrapped up in doing a perfect job that I can't let go and delegate things to others? Do my perfectionistic tendencies make me difficult to work with—always imposing my own excessively high standards on others and criticizing them when they can't meet my norms?

How do I deal with frustration, anger, and conflict in group enterprises? Suppress my feelings? Act out with aggression and hostility? Withdraw into isolation? Conform passively and swallow my feelings? Act out my anger with passive aggression by coming late to meetings, gossiping, spreading rumors, not meeting deadlines, etc.?

How do my own sexual feelings affect the way I work with others? Am I comfortable enough with my own sexual orientation and sexual feelings that I can work comfortably and closely with men and women, gays and straights—without anxiety and stress? Does my fear of intimacy inhibit my being a good team-player or do my unmet intimacy needs interfere with my working relationship with the staff?

These questions reflect the common human concerns that we bring with us wherever we go. When any of these issues—security, self-worth, anger, or sexuality—becomes problematic in ministry, it may mean that we are neglecting other areas of our life. Ministry can easily consume all the time and energy we have. Unless we learn to set limits, to give a fair share to other aspects of our life, we will not achieve the balance that a holistic spirituality seeks.

FOSTERING A CONTEMPLATIVE ATTITUDE

To achieve a balanced spirituality, a certain contemplative distance from our work is needed. We must have time and space to go apart and reflectively process our experiences of working together. Times for leisure and solitude must balance off times for work and community. There should be a rhythmic alternation between engagement and disengagement, involvement and withdrawal. When the apostles returned from their first missionary journey, Jesus led them off to a deserted place to rest and be together because they had been so busy that they had little time for anything but work (Mk 6:30-33). This kind of apostolic withdrawal is not an escape from ministry, but a necessary retreat that makes us more sensitively attuned to the voices that cry out for our attention. Paradoxically, being too close to a situation can sometimes deafen us to what is really going on, while standing apart can provide the contemplative distance that allows us to hear.

Contemplation, the still point in our fast-paced world that grounds meaning and purpose, is the foundation of a holistic spirituality. It provides the necessary space in our crowded lives for the essential, but often neglected, "activities of the whole, albeit, incomplete human person...for dreaming and desire, hunger and aspiration."[11] Contemplation is a way of connecting with our interior life, the flow of emotions, thoughts, sensations, desires, needs, wants, fantasies, urges that constitutes our subjectivity. The intimate self-knowledge that contemplation makes possible deepens our awareness of God's indwelling presence in our hearts and also makes us more conscious and responsible in our interactions with others. Contemplation is not an optional item on a list of things to do, but is rather the life breath of our compassionate outreach to others because, without it, we risk losing contact with God, others, and self.

"Get a Life!"

Having a personal life apart from our work, with ample time for family, friendship and leisure, is another important prerequisite for successful collaboration because it prevents the unhealthy fusion of personal identity and persona. When we identify ourselves with our jobs, many problems are likely to follow. Family and friendship give us a healthy sense of self and a security that comes from knowing that we are valued for ourselves, rather than for our achievements, performance, position, or power. While we never grow indifferent to personal success, the less its importance, the more collaborative enterprises thrive.

Overidentifying with our roles can lead to burnout because the nature of ministry is so open-ended that there are no clear limits.

There is always more to be done. If we do not cultivate a private life apart from our work, we can easily be consumed by it. In the old "western" movies, the saloon scene often showed a sign that read: "All guns must be checked at the door." Friendship, rest, and play that truly refreshes have one thing in common: all roles have to be checked at the door.

While genuine friendships may occasionally develop among colleagues, people working together in teams must not expect to have their intimacy needs met at work. Bernard Swain, director of a project in collaborative ministry, cites two dangers that result when the role of colleague or team member is not clearly distinguished from other roles. First, people may gravitate to team ministry "expecting an experience of, substitute for, or extension of family life, community life, or friendship."[12] These unrealistic expectations of collaboration lead to frustration and disappointment. Second, ministers otherwise attracted to team ministry may avoid it because they think that "team" means becoming close friends or family to each other; and this is more than they are prepared to give. For these reasons, Swain concludes, those training for team ministry "should be formed in a role that does not need—and should not expect—to depend on colleagues becoming friends, family, or community."[13]

PERFECTIONISM IMPEDES COLLABORATION

Striving for perfection, when it drives us to overwork and results in chronic fatigue, can also be an obstacle to effective collaboration. Ironically, when we strain to do everything perfectly, we undermine ourselves in several ways. First, severe and continual pressure leads to exhaustion, distaste for our work, and eventually to poor performance. To improve effectiveness, we who find ourselves working compulsively are challenged not to care less passionately about our work, but to relax our efforts and to be gently accepting of ourselves when we fall short. Second, perfectionistic tendencies handicap our ability to work with others. Already tired and cramped for time, we find that meetings, an essential component of collaboration, become a nuisance and collaborating with others undesirable. Third, the need to have everything done perfectly makes us reluctant to delegate, because others may not meet our standards. This inability to trust others may isolate us so that we eventually operate as lone rangers rather than as collaborators.

Perfectionists have a negative impact on others. Like the Pharisees, they lay heavy burdens on those with whom they work. Karen Horney describes how the drive for perfection is externalized and imposed on others: "[This] person may primarily impose his standards upon others and make relentless demands as to their perfection. The more he feels himself the measure of all things, the more he insists...not upon general perfection but upon his particular norms being measured up to. The failure of others to do so arouses his contempt or anger."[14] Horney's description can serve as a warning against putting excessive expectations on coworkers. If our colleagues are already perfection-prone and themselves given to overwork, what they need is not reinforcement of their compulsion, but help in understanding their limitations and accepting their humanness.

THE WAY OF EFFORTLESS ACTION

While perfectionism causes us to push and strain, the Taoist concept of wu-wei encourages us not to force things, but instead to go with the grain, to roll with the punch, to swim with the current. Wu-wei, or the way of "non-doing," stems from Lao-tzu's famous words: "The Tao does nothing, and yet nothing is left undone."[15] Believers of Taoism know that these words are not to be taken literally or used to justify inertia, laziness, laissez-faire, or irresponsible passivity. Rather, wu-wei encourages relaxed and focused effort.

Where perfectionism is rigid, wu-wei is flexible. Philosopher Alan Watts illustrates the way of non-doing with a comparison between a pine branch, which is hard and stiff, and a willow branch, which is soft and springy. In a winter storm, the heavy snow gathers on the pine branch until the mounting weight causes it to snap. The willow branch, on the other hand, yields to the weight of the snow and lets itself get pressed to the ground, where it is able to gracefully unload its oppressive burden and spring back to its natural position.[16] Of course, the willow's way is the path of effortless action.

A Taoist tale, entitled "Cutting Up an Ox," shows how wu-wei encourages a contemplative approach to action, especially when we are confronted with resistance.[17] The story is about a butcher who was so skillful at his craft that he used the same cleaver for nineteen years and managed to keep it as keen as if newly sharpened. When questioned about how he was able to cut up so many carcasses without dulling the blade, the butcher responded:

> There are spaces in the joints;
> The blade is thin and keen:
> When this thinness
> Finds that space
> There is all the room you need!
> It goes like a breeze!
> Hence I have this cleaver nineteen years
> As if newly sharpened!
>
> True, there are sometimes
> Tough joints. I feel them coming.
> I slow down, I watch closely,
> Hold back, barely move the blade,
> And whump! the part falls away.
> Then I withdraw the blade,
> I stand still
> And let the joy of the work
> Sink in.
> I clean the blade
> And put it away.

Unlike this wise butcher, perfectionists tend to speed up their pace and double their efforts when faced with opposition and hindrance. Instead of relying on force, *wu-wei* suggests that we slow down, hold back, and watch closely when encountering the "tough joints" in our lives. Only such a contemplative approach will allow us to see the "spaces" that will welcome our efforts.

In the arena of human action, *wu-wei* is a form of intelligence that allows a person who understands the dynamics of human affairs to use the least amount of energy to deal with them. This intelligence is not simply intellectual, states Watts, but also the "unconscious intelligence of the whole organism and, in particular, the innate wisdom of the nervous system. *Wu-wei* is a combination of this wisdom with taking the line of least resistance in all one's actions."[18]

Thomas Merton, who was a devotee of Taoist wisdom, renders his own version of a traditional Taoist story that reveals the essence of *wu-wei*:

When we wear out our minds, stubbornly clinging to one partial view of things, refusing to see a deeper agreement between this and its complementary opposite, we have what is called "three in the morning."

What is this "three in the morning"?

A monkey trainer went to his monkeys and told them: "As regards your chestnuts: you are going to have three measures in the morning and four in the afternoon."

At this they all became angry. So he said: "All right, in that case I will give you four in the morning and three in the afternoon." This time they were satisfied.

The two arrangements were the same in that the number of chestnuts did not change. But in one case the animals were displeased, and in the other they were satisfied. The keeper had been willing to change his personal arrangement in order to meet objective conditions. He lost nothing by it![19]

This story nicely illustrates the wisdom of *wu-wei*. The keeper had enough sense to recognize that the monkeys had their own reasons for wanting four measures of chestnuts in the morning, and he wasted neither time nor energy in stubbornly clinging to his original arrangement. By letting go, he was able to see things in perspective. And his accommodation to the monkeys only caused an accidental change, without affecting the substance of his arrangement.

A Christian understanding of *wu-wei* is reflected in the popular phrase, "Let go and let God." This wise saying encourages us to trust more deeply in the grace of God at work in our lives and to serenely let go of things that we cannot change at the present time. The path of *wu-wei* is based on the belief that the Tao, the principle of reality, is ultimately benevolent; thus we do not have to resist, or meddle, or interfere with the flow of life. Similarly, "letting go and letting God" rests on the conviction of faith that for those who love God, "all things work together unto good" (Rom 8:28). Of course, this faith relies on a contemplative attitude that recognizes God at work in all reality, laboring for our welfare. Christian faith reassures us that because God raised Jesus from the dead, reality is ultimately gracious and God can be trusted. Thus, Christians are called to trust in the provident love of God and to go with the flow of God's grace, which "can do infinitely more than we can ask or imagine"

(Eph 3:20-21). Trust in God resembles more the peaceful effort of *wu-wei* than the obsessive-compulsive way of perfectionism.

The New Testament concept of time as *kairos*, the fruitful time, the fullness of time, or the graced moment, also recommends the path of *wu-wei* in all we do. In contrast to time as *chronos*, which is linear or clock time, *kairos* conveys a specialness, the moment waited for when God's intervention on our behalf will become abundantly clear. *Kairos* encourages us not to be pushy, but to be patient; it invites us not to run ahead of grace. The following story illustrates the meaning of *kairos* and the kind of surrender based on trust required of us if we are to let go and let God.

> My father was dying; my mother was panicking. They were three thousand miles away from me. I had a family and a job. And all the familiar questions of these experiences: when to be with them, when to be at home and at work; when to call, when to wait to be called, medical decisions; hospital or home; and simply what to say, how to be.
>
> I'd think and think about all this, but I would reach a point where I'd see I had to stop. My mind would go "tilt." So I would go out and take a walk, or watch the river change tides and empty into the Atlantic. I'd watch kids at the playground. I'd see how the tree line had changed shape at the top of a mountain meadow I'd known for years. Things like that.
>
> And sometimes I'd hear: "Right. It's time to be out there. I'll leave in two weeks and stay ten days." Or, "Not so much advice giving." Or "God is with them." The right thought. Something that would ring true. These seemed to come out of the blue, but I felt trust in them, and peaceful as a result.
>
> It was very reliable and very inspiring, working that way. All through his illness and all the wild, anxious phone calls, I'd feel answers coming. It was very reassuring. I experienced it as grace. And at the end I was able to be with them at home and have his hand in mine as he died and my arm around my mother.[20]

In sum, *wu-wei* counters the obstacles to collaboration created by perfectionism by making us more relaxed, trusting, and patient in our work with others.

THE CALL OF WEAK AND WOUNDED PEOPLE

Scripture demonstrates that God has a history of calling weak and wounded people to embody divine compassion for those in need. When called, Moses complained to Yahweh, "Who am I to go to Pharaoh and bring the sons of Israel out of Egypt?" (Ex 3:11). "Never in my life have I been a man of eloquence, either before or since you have spoken to your servant. I am a slow speaker and not able to speak well.... If it please you, my Lord...send anyone you will!" (Ex 4:10-11, 13). "I shall be with you," was the answer given by Yahweh (Ex 3:12).

In a similar way, the prophet Jeremiah protested when God called him to serve: "Ah, Lord Yahweh; look, I do not know how to speak: I am a child!" "Ah, Ah, Ah, Lord": The Hebrew text suggests a stuttering, stammering quality to Jeremiah's fearful response (Jer 1:6). But Yahweh replied, "Do not say, 'I am a child.' Go now to those to whom I send you and say whatever I command you. Do not be afraid of them, for I am with you to protect you—it is Yahweh who speaks!" (Jer 1:7-8).

Luke's gospel shows Peter, tired because he fished all night and caught nothing, also trying to back off from a call to ministry. After the miraculous catch of fish, he fell at the knees of Jesus saying, "Leave me, Lord; I am a sinful man." To which Jesus responded, "Do not be afraid; from now on it is people you will catch" (Lk 5:8-9, 10-11).

The biblical pattern that emerges from these texts seems to be this: first, God takes the initiative in inviting people to serve. Second, those called express a sense of personal inadequacy. Third, there is an experience of being touched. Fourth, there is the divine reassurance of God's strength and protection. This biblical pattern can help us understand better what our call to ministry today entails: to hear the invitation as Christians to embody the compassion of Jesus in the world; to admit that we are weak and wounded healers; to experience God's presence with us in ministry; and, finally, to rely on God's power always at work in all we do. Only a contemplative attitude can enable us to do this.

WEAKNESS AND EFFECTIVE MINISTRY

Instead of being an obstacle, the experience of weakness is an important condition for effective ministry. Personal weakness disposes us to open ourselves to being helped and supported. It cultivates a sense of humility and poverty of spirit that welcomes collaboration. Conversely, knowing our own need for support, we are more attuned to how our coworkers might also need assistance. This awareness strengthens collaboration by making us more understanding and sensitive to the needs of colleagues. Finally, personal struggles and weakness expand our capacity for compassion by forming an experiential basis in our hearts for feeling for and with people. Our own vulnerability gives us empathic knowledge of the pain that others may be feeling. Paradoxically, weakness strengthens us in ministry when it keeps us open to our need for collaborating with others and reminds us that our effectiveness ultimately depends on God's grace.

When discouraged by the complex challenge of making collaboration work, we, like Moses, Jeremiah, and Peter, can find reassurance in God's promise to be powerfully with us as we go forth to do God's work. Our felt weakness, even though painful at times, keeps us always mindful of our need to rely more on God's power than on our own resources. Since ministry is God's saving activity in the world today, its success ultimately depends on God. After unsuccessfully begging God three times to have a troubling weakness, a "thorn in the flesh," taken away, Paul was told by God, "My grace is enough for you; my power is at its best in weakness" (2 Cor 12:9). This divine reassurance elicits a trusting response from Paul: "So I shall be very happy to make my weaknesses my special boast so that the power of Christ may stay over me, and that is why I am quite content with my weakness, and with insults, hardships, persecutions, and the agonies I go through for Christ's sake. For it is when I am weak that I am strong" (2 Cor 12:9-10).

Reflection Questions

1. Discuss: "Collaboration is the movement from competition to contemplation." What concrete implications would this statement have for your work in embodying the compassion of God for others?

2. What in you fosters collaborative efforts? What in you hinders collaborative efforts?

3. How do you experience weakness in your work and ministry? What are concrete ways in which colleagues and partners can support you? What are concrete ways in which you can offer support to them?

EPILOGUE: TO HAVE,
TO HOLD, AND TO HAND OVER

A JOYOUS HOMECOMING happens when all the aspects of who we are find a peaceful acceptance in us, allowing us to feel a sense of wholeness. As this process of self-acceptance deepens, our shameful feeling of being defective and unlovable shrinks and is replaced by humility, a deep realization that who we are *at the present moment* is good enough to warrant our own joyful embrace and also good enough to be held in existence by God's sustaining love. Humility eliminates our anxious need to be perfect and moves us to gratefully accept ourselves as creatures: limited, yet good; sinful, yet loved.

Like the prodigal son who made his tortuous way home feeling unworthy and ashamed, we too are called to effect a fundamental shift in attitude toward ourselves: to move from a self-rejection based on envious comparisons with others to a self-acceptance filled with gratitude for our many blessings. The prodigal son, being so exuberantly held by his welcoming father, must have felt deep in his bones that it was okay to be his weak and unsure self— okay, too, to trust in his father's faithful love as he integrated the lessons of his painful past to guide his future. Jesus used the parable of the prodigal son to provide a glimpse of the immensity of God's love, which embraces the totality of our being, shadow and all. Throughout the seasons of our lives, the God who causes the sun to shine on the good and the bad and lets the rain fall on the just and the unjust never fails to bathe our existence with abundant grace and acceptance.

Conversion requires us, in imitation of God, to lovingly accept ourselves without condition. Or as theologian Paul Tillich put it in describing faith, to have "the courage to accept our acceptability despite feelings of unacceptability."[1] Too often, we withhold love from ourselves and place a myriad of conditions on our lovableness. A voice within us says, "I would be lovable, *if only* I were more attractive, intelligent, gifted, successful, and so on." This same voice drives us to overwork in an anxious search for material goods and accomplishments that we hope will secure our well-being and reflect our goodness to others. In contrast, the gospel message teaches us that the voice we need to heed is the heavenly voice that addressed Jesus in the Jordan and seeks to convey the same divine affirmation to each of us today: "*You* are my beloved one in whom I take great delight." Only when we allow this divine affirmation to permeate our hearts and to reverberate throughout our being will we experience that personal solidity that comes from being rooted in God's unconditional love. God's love not only makes us come to be, but also makes us good *in our very being*. While the praise and esteem of others may be declarative of our goodness, God's love alone is constitutive of our goodness. In other words, God's love for us is foundational because it both establishes us in life and causes us to be lovable. Peaceful acceptance of ourselves will come when we *experience*, with felt knowledge, the fact that we are loved by God insofar as we exist and not for any of our personal attributes or qualities, talents or accomplishments. Without this realization, self-rejection will forever feed our need to compensate for our inadequacy through codependent, perfectionistic, envious, and workaholic behaviors.

Embracing our existence as human beings is a necessary part of the process of becoming whole. This can be a mighty challenge especially for those of us who struggle with codependency, resulting from emotional abandonment and neglect in childhood. Psychiatrist Rollo May provides a poignant illustration of what the courage to be sometimes can entail in his account of a patient's "I-Am" experience.[2] This patient, an intelligent woman of twenty-eight, had come for psychotherapy because of serious anxieties in closed places and severe self-doubts. An illegitimate child, she was raised in an atmosphere of rejection. At troubled times, her mother, reminding her of her origin and recounting how she tried to abort her, would angrily shout at the girl: "If you hadn't been born, we wouldn't have to go through this!"

In the fourth month of her therapy, she dreamed that she was in a crowd of faceless people looking like shadows. "It seemed like a wilderness of people," she recounted. "Then I saw there was someone in the crowd who had compassion for me." In the session following that dream, she reported an exceedingly important experience.

I remember walking that day under the elevated tracks in a slum area, feeling the thought, "I am an illegitimate child." I recall the sweat pouring forth in my anguish in trying to accept that fact. Then I understood what it must feel like to accept.... "I am blind in the midst of people who see." Later on that night I woke up and it came to me this way, "I accept the fact that I am an illegitimate child." *But* "I am not a child anymore." So it is, "I am illegitimate." That is not so either: "I was born illegitimate." Then what is left? What is left is this, "*I Am.*" This *act* of contact and acceptance with "I am," once gotten hold of, gave me (what I think was for me the first time) the experience "Since I Am, I have the right to be."

What is this experience like? It is a primary feeling—it feels like receiving the deed to my house. It is the experience of my own aliveness not caring whether it turns out to be an ion or just a wave.... It is like a sailboat in the harbor being given an anchor so that, being made out of earthly things, it can by means of its anchor get in touch again with the earth, the ground from which its wood grew; it can lift its anchor to sail but always at times it can cast its anchor to weather the storm or rest a little....

...It is like the experience of the poets of the intuitive world, the mystics, except that instead of the pure feeling of and union with God it is the finding of and the union with my own being. It is like owning Cinderella's shoe and looking all over the world for the foot it will fit and realizing all of a sudden that one's own foot is the only one it will fit.... It is like a globe before the mountains and oceans and continents have been drawn on it. It is like a child in grammar finding the *subject* of the verb in a sentence—in this case the subject being one's own life span. It is ceasing to feel like a theory toward one's self....[3]

The "I-am" experience of this woman, in which her sense of being emerges and is strengthened, is vitally important for all of us, if we are to understand the fullness of God's love. The experience represented a dramatic moment of healing grace for her because of the patent threat to her being that she had suffered in childhood. While our early experience may not have been as invalidating and rejecting as hers, the human condition saddles all of us with a certain ontological anxiety about our adequacy and lovableness. And like May's patient, we need to be grasped by this central truth of faith: that since we are, we have the right to be, that God loves us in our "I-am-ness." Or as the book of Wisdom puts it: "Yes, you love all that exists, you hold nothing of what you have made in abhorrence, for had you hated anything, you would have not formed it. And how, had you not willed it, could a thing persist, how be conserved if not called forth by you? You spare all things because all things are yours, Lord, lover of life, you whose imperishable spirit is in all" (Wis 11:25-27).

Christian transformation requires both self-appropriation, the having and holding of a self, and self-transcendence, the handing over of our self to God and others in love. Love of self finds its fulfillment when we are able to wholeheartedly love God and our neighbor "as we love ourselves." As scholastic philosophy has long taught, love by its very nature extends itself. Our hard-won self-love becomes a source of life for others, forming the foundation for them to accept their lovableness. For any human being the possibility of self-acceptance requires the prior acceptance by a significant other. Importantly, May's patient's powerful experience of affirmation came after a dream in which she found one person in the barren wilderness of the crowd who had compassion for her. In a similar way, our compassionate love of others can be the graceful occasion when they are given an "I-am" experience, awaking in them an awareness of their radical acceptability. As the gracefulness of their own being dawns on them, they grow in self-love and gratefully extend this love to others, now handing over their being to God and neighbor, giving as they have received.

For most of us, self-esteem is something we hold tenuously. Moments of doubt make us forget the graciousness of our being, and we need to be reminded of our loveliness. Poet Galway Kinnell eloquently expresses the affirming nature of love in his account of St. Francis and the sow.

> The bud
> stands for all things
> even for those things that don't flower,
> for everything flowers, from within, of self-blessing;
> though sometimes it is necessary
> to reteach a thing its loveliness,
> to put a hand on its brow
> of the flower
> and retell it in words and in touch
> it is lovely
> until it flowers again from within, of self-blessing;
> as Saint Francis

put his hand on the creased forehead
of the sow, and told her in words and in touch
blessings of earth on the sow, and the sow
began remembering all down her thick length,
from the earthen snout all the way
through the fodder and slops
to the spiritual curl of the tail,
from hard spininess spiked out from the spine
down through the great broken heart
to the blue milken dreaminess spurting and shuddering
from the fourteen teats into the fourteen mouths sucking and
    blowing beneath them:
the long, perfect loveliness of sow.[4]

Finally, because the urgings of the human heart for wholeness and fulfillment can be satisfied by God alone, we need to hand ourselves over to God. As St. Augustine put it so beautifully, "You have made us for yourself, O God, and our hearts will remain restless until they rest in you." Yet, we are meant to be with God even now, at every moment of our lives. That is why Jesuit poet Gerard Manley Hopkins tells us to hand over our life—with all its worries and struggles, delights and beauty—to God's keeping and to give it now:

    deliver it, early now, long before death
Give beauty back, beauty, beauty, beauty, back to
    God, beauty's self and beauty's giver.
See; not a hair is, not an eyelash, not the least lash lost;
    every hair
Is, hair of the head, numbered.[5]

NOTES

Introduction

1. See Stephen Arterburn and Jack Felton, *Faith That Hurts, Faith That Heals* (Nashville, TN: Oliver-Nelson, 1993).

2. Ruth Burrows, *Before the Living God* (London: Sheed & Ward, 1975), 118.

3. St Irenaeus, *Adversus Haereses* IV, 20, 7.

4. Anthony de Mello, S.J., *One Minute Wisdom* (Garden City, NY: Doubleday & Company, Inc., 1986), 10.

Chapter One

1. Neils Bohr as quoted in Parker J. Palmer, *The Active Life: A Spirituality of Work, Creativity, and Caring* (San Francisco, CA: Harper & Row, 1990), 15.

2. Neil Micklem, "The Shadow of Wholeness," *Harvest: Journal for Jungian Studies* 39 (1993):115.

3. Expressions such as "the way of the Lord" (18:25), "the way of salvation" (16:17) and especially "the way," are also found in Acts to refer to those who follow in the footsteps of Jesus Christ (9:2; 18:26; 19:9, 23; 22:4; 24:14, 22).

4. Anonymous in *The Sower's Seeds: One Hundred Inspiring Stories for Preaching, Teaching and Public Speaking*, ed. Brian Cavanaugh, T.O.R. (Mahwah, NJ: Paulist Press, 1990), 58-60.

5. Thomas Merton, *Life and Holiness* (New York: Herder and Herder, 1963), 18-19.

6. Josef Goldbrunner, *Holiness Is Wholeness and Other Essays* (Notre Dame, IN: The Notre Dame University Press, 1964), 38.

7. William Silverman, *Rabbinic Wisdom and Jewish Values*, rev. ed. (New York: Union of American Hebrew Congregations, 1971), 74.

8. Josef Goldbrunner, *Holiness Is Wholeness*, 38.

9. Michael J. Buckley, S.J., *The Berkeley Jesuit*, 1 (Spring 1970):7.

10. Anthony de Mello, S.J., *One Minute Wisdom* (Garden City, NY: Doubleday & Company, 1986), 91.

11. Ibid., 67.

12. Lawrence Jaffe, *Liberating the Heart: Spirituality and Jungian Psychology* (Toronto: Inner City Books, 1990), 84.

13. John Sanford, *Healing and Wholeness* (New York: Paulist Press, 1977), 20.

14. Thomas Keating, *Invitation to Love: The Way of Christian Contemplation* (Rockport, MA: St. Benedict's Monastery, 1992), 12.

15. Parker J. Palmer, *The Active Life: A Spirituality of Work, Creativity, and Caring* (San Francisco: Harper & Row, 1990), 27.

16. Thomas Keating, *Invitation to Love*, 2.

17. Steve Payne, "The Dark Night of St. John of the Cross: Four Centuries Later," *Review for Religious* (November/December 1990):898.

18. Ibid., 897.

19. Gerard W. Hughes, S.J., *God of Surprises* (Mahwah, NJ: Paulist Press, 1985), x.

Chapter Two

1. C. G. Jung, *Dreams*, trans. R. F. C. Hull (Princeton, NJ: Princeton University Press, 1974), 233.

2. Thomas Keating, *Open Mind, Open Heart: The Contemplative Dimension of the Gospel* (Amity, NY: Amity House, 1986), 15.

3. Robert Bly, *A Little Book on the Shadow*, ed. William Booth (San Francisco: Harper & Row, 1988), 19.

4. See Alice Miller's books, *The Drama of the Gifted Child* (New York: Basic Books, 1981), *For Your Own Good: Hidden Cruelty in Child-Rearing and the Roots of Violence* (New York: Farrar, Straus & Giroux, 1983), *Thou Shalt Not Be Aware: Society's Betrayal of the Child* (New York: New American Library, 1984), and *Pictures of a Childhood* (New York: Farrar, Straus & Giroux, 1986).

5. David Steindl-Rast, "The Shadow in Christianity," in *Meeting the Shadow: The Hidden Power of the Dark Side of Human Nature*, ed. Connie Zweig and Jeremiah Abrams (Los Angeles: Jeremy P. Tarcher, 1991), 131-32.

6. C. G. Jung, *Collected Works* (Bollingen Series XX), Vol. 16. trans. R. F. C. Hull and ed. H. Read, M. Fordham, G. Adler, and William McGuire (Princeton, NJ: Princeton University Press) 389.

7. Joanie Albrecht, "Addiction to Light: Fundamentalism and the Denial of Shadow," *Psychological Perspectives* 27 (Fall/Winter 1992):41.

8. David Lowell Kern, "Greeting the Shadow That Lives Down the Road," *Psychological Perspectives* 27 (Fall/Winter 1992):110-111.

9. Ibid., 113.

10. William Miller, *Your Golden Shadow: Discovering and Fulfilling Your Undeveloped Self* (San Francisco: HarperSanFrancisco, 1989), 59.

11. The meaning of dream images of the opposite sex is discussed in Chapter Seven under the topic, "Animus/Anima Projections."

12. Charles H. Klaif, "Emerging Concepts of the Self: Clinical Considerations," in *Archetypal Processes in Psychotherapy* (Los Angeles: Chiron Publications, 1987), 86-87.

13. Vernon E. Brooks, "What Does Analytical Psychology Offer Those with No Access to Analysis?" *Quadrant* 8, no. 2 (Winter 1975):127.

Chapter Three

1. Virginia Curran Hoffman, *The Codependent Church* (New York: The Crossroad Publishing Company, 1991), 15f.

2. Melody Beattie, *Codependent No More* (New York: Harper & Row, 1987), 7.

3. Martin W. Pable, O.F.M. Cap., "Psychology and Asceticism of Celibacy," *Review for Religious* 34, no. 2 (1975):271.

4. Judith R. Brown, *"I Only Want What's Best for You": A Parent's Guide to Raising Emotionally Healthy Children* (New York: St. Martin's Press, 1986), 8.

5. Richard Neuhaus, "The Gospel of Therapy," *First Things* 7 (November 1990):68.

6. Dale E. Larsen, "Codependent Caregiving," *Santa Clara Magazine* (Summer 1991): 46.

7. This excerpt from *Emphasis–A Preaching Journal for the Parish Pastor*, C.S.S. Publishing Co., Lima, OH, 14, no. 4, 4.

8. William B. Spohn, S.J. "The Biblical Theology of the Pastoral Letter and Ignatian Contemplation," *Studies in the Spirituality of American Jesuits*, Vol. 17, No. 4 (St. Louis: The American Seminar on Jesuit Spirituality, 1985), 8-9.

9. For further information regarding the concept of the inner child, see W. Hugh Missildine, M.D., *Your Inner Child of the Past* (New York: Pocket Books, 1963) and Eric Berne, M.D., *Games People Play* (New York: Ballantine Books, 1964).

10. *Today's Headlines* (newsletter of Daniel Freeman Hospitals, Los Angeles, CA), 6 April 1994.

Chapter Four

1. Leo Rock, S.J., *Making Friends with Yourself: Christian Growth and Self-Acceptance* (Mahwah, NJ: Paulist Press, 1990), 99.

2. Asher R. Pacht, "Reflections on Perfection," *American Psychologist* (April 1984):387.

3. Ben Sorotzkin, "The Quest for Perfection: Avoiding Guilt or Avoiding Shame?" *Psychotherapy* 22, no. 3 (Fall 1985):564-65.

4. D. Louise Mebane and Charles R. Ridley, "The Role-Sending of Perfectionism: Overcoming Counterfeit Spirituality," *Journal of Psychology and Theology* 16, no. 4 (1988):335.

5. Ibid.

6. Joseph N. Tylenda, S.J., *Jesuit Saints and Martyrs: Short Biographies of the Saints, Blessed, Venerables, and Servants of God of the Society of Jesus* (Chicago: Loyola University Press, 1984), 429.

7. David D. Burns, "The Perfectionist's Script for Self-Defeat," *Psychology Today*, November 1980, 34.

8. Sorotzkin, "The Quest for Perfection," 565.

9. Marion Woodman, *Addiction to Perfection: The Still Unravished Bride* (Toronto: Inner City Books, 1982), 10.

10. Randie L. Timpe, "Perfectionism: Positive Possibility or Personal Pathology," *Journal of Psychology and Christianity* 82, no. 2 (Summer 1989):24-28.

11. Karen Horney, *The Neurotic Personality of Our Time* (New York: W. W. Norton & Company, 1937), 84.

12. Karen Horney, *Neurosis and Human Growth* (New York: W. W. Norton & Company, 1950), 64-65.

13. Sorotzkin, "The Quest for Perfection," 567.

14. Although real-life perfectionists usually have both neurotic and narcissistic aspects, it is important to keep this distinction in mind when working with perfectionists in counseling or spiritual direction. In the case of neurotic perfectionism, helpers need to assist clients to examine and modify their excessively high ideals, bringing them into line with what is more humanly possible. The goal here is the gradual transformation of a harsh superego into a healthy moral conscience. This approach, however, would be too threatening to those whose perfectionism is more narcissistic in nature because, in this case, being perfect is the glue that holds their identity intact. Here a more fruitful strategy would be to foster the development of a healthy, differentiated sense of self, capable of self-love and self-direction. Narcissistic perfectionists need to be continually reassured about their own goodness, since this is what was lacking in their childhood. An outgrowth of such remedial ego formation is the gradual defining of morals and ideals that are personal and internalized.

Helpers can unwittingly fail to provide adequate and accurate empathy when they do not properly distinguish between these two types of perfectionism. Challenging narcissistic perfectionists on their perfectionism is counterproductive because it would be experienced as an attack on the self and, as such, a painful rejection. Empathic confrontation, however, is helpful when challenging the severe and unrealistic demands of neurotic perfectionists. As in all helping relationships, empathic attunement is at the heart of healing and transformation.

15. Johannes B. Metz, *Poverty of Spirit*, trans. John Drury (Mahwah, NJ: Paulist Press, 1968), 7.

16. P. Beck and D. Burns, "Anxiety and Depression in Law Students: Cognitive Intervention," *Journal of Legal Education* 30 (1979):270-90.

17. Richard Driscoll, "Self-Condemnation: A Comprehensive Framework for Assessment and Treatment," *Psychotherapy*, 26, no. 1 (Spring 1989):108.

18. D. Louise Mebane and Charles R. Ridley, "The Role-Sending of Perfectionism," 335-37.

19. William A. Spohn, S.J., "The Moral Vision of the Catechism: Thirty Years That Did Not Happen," *America*, 3 March 1990, 192.

20. William Barclay, *The Gospel of Matthew* (Philadelphia: Westminster Press, 1956), 175, 177.

21. William Spohn, S.J., "The Moral Vision of the Catechism," 192.

22. C. G. Jung, *Collected Works, Aion* (Bollingen Series XX), trans. R. F. C. Hull and ed. H. Read, M. Fordham, G. Adler, and William McGuire (Princeton, NJ: Princeton University Press) 9ii, par. 123.

23. Taken from Wilkie Au, *By Way of the Heart: Toward a Holistic Christian Spirituality* (Mahwah, NJ: Paulist Press, 1989), 137-39.

Chapter Five

1. Horace, *Epistles*, book 1, i, line 58.

2. Moshe Haim Luzzatto, *The Path of the Just*, trans. Shraga Silverstein, Feldheim, 1966, as quoted in Solomon Schimmel, *The Seven Deadly Sins: Jewish, Christian, and Classical Reflections on Human Nature* (New York: The Free Press, 1992), 60.

3. This illustration has been adapted from an account in Solomon Schimmel, *The Seven Deadly Sins: Jewish, Christian, and Classical Reflections on Human Nature* (New York: The Free Press, 1992), 56-57.

4. Melanie Klein, *Envy and Gratitude: A Study of Unconscious Sources* (London: Tavistock Publications, 1957), 1-91.

5. Ann and Barry Ulanov, *Cinderella and Her Sisters: The Envied and the Envying* (Philadelphia: Westminster Press, 1983), 83.

6. Ibid., 97.

7. Johannes Metz, *Poverty of Spirit* (New York: Paulist Press, 1968), 7.

Chapter Six

1. Bruce Shackleton, "Meeting the Shadow at Work," in *Meeting the Shadow: The Hidden Power of the Dark Side of Human Nature*, ed. Connie Zweig and Jeremiah Abrams (Los Angeles: Jeremy P. Tarcher, Inc., 1991), 106.

2. Parker J. Palmer, *The Active Life: A Spirituality of Work, Creativity, and Caring* (San Francisco: Harper & Row, 1990), 10.

3. Connie Zweig and Jeremiah Abrams, *Meeting the Shadow*, 104.

4. "Ironically, the tendency of capitalism to expand work is often associated with a growth in joblessness. In recent years, as a majority have taken on the extra month of work, nearly one-fifth of all participants in the labor force are unable to secure as many hours as they want or need to make ends meet. While many employees are subjected to mandatory overtime and are suffering from overwork, their coworkers are put on involuntary part-time." Juliet B. Schor, *The Overworked American: The Unexpected Decline of Leisure* (New York: HarperCollins, 1991), 7.

5. Ibid., 5.

6. Ronald Yates, "Japanese Live...and Die...for Their Work," *Chicago Tribune*, 13 November 1988, 1.

7. Anthony de Mello, S.J., *The Song of the Bird* (Garden City, NY: Image Books/Doubleday & Company, 1984), 8.

8. John Grisham, *The Client* (New York: Doubleday, 1993), 183.

9. Daniel Rodgers, cited in Schor, *The Overworked American*, 70.

10. It has been suggested by Michael J. Buckley, S.J., Director of the Jesuit Institute at Boston College, in a private conversation, that this prayer for generosity, traditionally attributed to St. Ignatius of Loyola, did not originate with Ignatius, but was composed in the nineteenth century for sodalists.

11. Diane Fassel, *Working Ourselves to Death: The High Cost of Workaholism, The Rewards of Recovery* (San Francisco: HarperSanFrancisco, 1990), 11.

12. Ibid., 30.

13. Schor, *The Overworked American*, p. 89.

14. This example is based on a case cited by Fassel in *Working Ourselves to Death*, 17-18.

15. Carmen Renee Berry, *When Helping You Is Hurting Me: Escaping the Messiah Trap* (San Francisco: Harper & Row, 1988), 6-7.

16. Thomas Frazier, "Dysfunctions in Ministry," *Human Development*, 13, no. 1 (Spring 1992):8.

17. Schor, *The Overworked American*, 3.

18. This example is cited by Fassel in *Working Ourselves to Death*, 56.

19. Schor, *The Overworked American*, 4. Arguing that leisure has been a

conspicuous casualty of prosperity, Schor reports that "in 1990, the average American owns and consumes more than twice as much as he or she did in 1948, but also has less free time" (p. 2).

20. Ibid., 114.

21. Ibid., 158.

22. Overwork is rampant among the nation's poorly-paid workers. Schor succinctly depicts their plight: "At $5, $6, or even $7 an hour, annual earnings before taxes and deductions range from $10,000 to $14,000. Soaring rents alone have been enough to put many of these low earners in financial jeopardy. For the more than one-third of all workers now earning hourly wages of $7 and below, the pressure to lengthen hours has been inexorable." Ibid., 21-22.

23. Brian Cavanaugh, T.O.R., *The Sower's Seeds: One Hundred Inspiring Stories for Preaching, Teaching and Public Speaking* (Mahwah, NJ: Paulist Press, 1990), 56.

24. Joan Chittister, OSB, *Wisdom Distilled from the Daily: Living the Rule of St. Benedict Today* (New York: HarperCollins, 1990), 98.

25. Abad-Ha-am's encomium on the sabbath, quoted in Thomas Hicks' "The Sabbath Rediscovered," *America*, 11 July 1992, 16.

Chapter Seven

1. Rainer Maria Rilke, *Letters to a Young Poet*, trans. M. D. Herter (New York: W. W. Norton, 1963) 53-54.

2. Raymond E. Brown, S.S., "Gospel of John (i-xii): Introduction, Translation and Notes," in *The Anchor Bible*, Vol. 29 (Garden City, NY: Doubleday & Company, 1966), 17.

3. Ibid., xciv.

4. C. G. Jung, *The Development of Personality: Papers on Child Psychology, Education, and Related Subjects*, trans. R. F. C. Hull (Princeton, NJ: Princeton University Press, 1981), 198.

5. John Sanford, *The Invisible Partners* (Mahwah, NJ: Paulist Press, 1980), 19.

6. For further discussion of active imagination, see John Sanford, *The Invisible Partners*, 119-28.

7. John Welwood, *Journey of the Heart: Intimate Relationships and the Path of Love* (New York: HarperCollins Publishers, 1990), 99.

8. Verena Kast, *The Nature of Loving: Family, Friendship, Marriage* (Wilmette, IL: Chiron Press, 1986), 84.

9. Adolf Guggenbühl-Craig, *Marriage–Dead or Alive*, trans. Murray Stein (Zürich, Switzerland: Spring Publications, 1977).

10. Andrew M. Greeley, *The Cardinal Virtues* (New York: Warner Books, 1990), 391-94.

11. *Life as Prayer and Other Writings of Evelyn Underhill*, ed. Lucy Menzies (Harrisburg, PA: Morehouse Publishing, 1991), 23.

12. Monika K. Hellwig, "A Royal Priesthood," *America*, 9 May 1987, 393.

13. Ibid.

14. Belden C. Lane, "Rabbinical Stories: A Primer on Theological Method," *Christian Century*, 16 December 1981, 1307-08.

Chapter Eight

1. D. P. McNeill, D. A. Morrison, and H. J. M. Nouwen, *Compassion: A Reflection on the Christian Life* (New York: Doubleday & Company, 1981), 50, 51.

2. Edward J. Mally, S.J., "The Gospel According to Mark," *The Jerome Biblical Commentary* (Englewood Cliffs, NJ: Prentice-Hall, Inc., 1968), Vol. II:35.

3. St. Ignatius of Loyola, *The Spiritual Exercises of St. Ignatius*, ed. L. J. Puhl (Chicago: Loyola University Press, 1951), #103.

4. Parker J. Palmer, *The Active Life: A Spirituality of Work, Creativity, and Care* (San Francisco: Harper & Row, 1990), 130.

5. Ibid.

6. D. P. McNeill, D. A. Morrison, and H. J. M. Nouwen, *Compassion*, 57.

7. Adapted from Brian Cavanaugh, *More Sower's Seeds: Second Planting* (Mahwah, NJ: Paulist Press, 1992), 37.

8. *Spiritual Exercises*, #236.

9. It is sometimes argued, even by Jesuits themselves, that Ignatius said just the opposite: "Pray as if everything depends on God; work as if everything depends on you." However, Jesuit theologian Francis Smith asserts "We now know that...the correct version in a simplified form" is "Pray as if everything depends on you; act as if everything depends on God." In its full form, translated from the Latin, Ignatius said, "Have faith in God, as if all success depended on you, nothing on God; set to work, however, as if nothing were to come about through you, and everything through God alone." According to Smith, "One could debate what the fuller version means, but...I think the simplified version is an accurate capturing of its meaning." Francis R. Smith, S.J., "The Religious Experience of Ignatius of Loyola and the Mission of Jesuit Higher Education Today" (paper presented at the Fourth Institute on Jesuit Higher Education, University of San Francisco, San Francisco, CA, June 6-9, 1990), 2-3.

10. Joseph de Guibert, S.J., *The Jesuits: Their Spiritual Doctrine and Practice* (St. Louis: The Institute of Jesuit Sources, 1964), 38-39.

11. John F. Kavanaugh, "Time to Stand and Stare," *The Way: Contemporary Christian Spirituality* 23, no. 3 (July 1983):211.

12. Bernard Swain, *Liberating Leadership: Practical Styles for Pastoral Ministry* (San Francisco: Harper & Row, 1986), 119.

13. Ibid.

14. Karen Horney, *Neurosis and Human Growth* (New York: Norton, 1950), 78.

15. As quoted in Alan Watts, *Tao: The Watercourse Way* (New York: Pantheon Books/Random House, 1975), 75.

16. Ibid., 76.

17. Thomas Merton, *The Way of Chuang Tzu* (New York: New Dimensions, 1969), 45-47.

18. Alan Watts, *Tao: The Watercourse Way*, 76.

19. Thomas Merton, *The Way of Chuang Tzu*, 44.

20. Baba Ram Dass and Paul Gorman, *How Can I Help?: Stories and Reflections on Service* (New York: Alfred A. Knopf, 1985), 110.

Epilogue

1. Paul Tillich, *The Courage to Be* (New Haven: Yale University Press, 1952), 164-65, 172-73.

2. Rollo May, "Contributions of Existential Psychotherapy," in *Existence: A New Dimension in Psychiatry and Psychology*, ed. Rollo May, Ernest Angel, and Henri F. Ellenberger (New York: Basic Books, 1958), 42-43.

3. Ibid., 43.

4. Galway Kinnel, "St. Francis and the Sow," in *Mortal Acts, Mortal Words* (Boston: Houghton Mifflin Company, 1980), 9.

5. Gerard Manley Hopkins, "The Leaden Echo and the Golden Echo," in *Poems and Prose of Gerard Manley Hopkins*, ed. W. H. Gardner (Baltimore, MD: Penguin Books, Inc., 1953), 53-54.

INDEX